Mihnea Tănăsescu
Understanding the Rights of Nature

New Ecology | Volume 6

Mihnea Tănăsescu, born in 1984, is a political ecologist with a background in human ecology, philosophy, and political science. He has published widely on the political representation of other than human beings. He was a research fellow of the Research Foundation Flanders (FWO) and a visiting fellow at the University of Auckland, NZ (Law), and the New School for Social Research, USA (Politics).

Mihnea Tănăsescu

Understanding the Rights of Nature

A Critical Introduction

[transcript]

The research for and writing of this book was made possible by generous funding from Research Foundation – Flanders (FWO), grants FWOKN317 and FWOTM756, and Evaluating Democratic Governance in Europe (EDGE) Research Program, Vrije Universiteit Brussel (VUB).

Bibliographic information published by the Deutsche Nationalbibliothek
The Deutsche Nationalbibliothek lists this publication in the Deutsche Nationalbibliografie; detailed bibliographic data are available in the Internet at http://dnb.d-nb.de

Cover layout: Maria Arndt, Bielefeld
Printed by Majuskel Medienproduktion GmbH, Wetzlar
Print-ISBN 978-3-8376-5431-8
PDF-ISBN 978-3-8394-5431-2
https://doi.org/10.14361/9783839454312
ISSN of series: 2569-7900
eISSN of series: 2703-1039

Printed on permanent acid-free text paper.

Contents

Acknowledgments

Many people have graciously given their time to making this work better. In no particular order, I want to thank Katherine Sanders, which hosted me at the University of Auckland Faculty of Law for a fruitful three months during which this book was conceived; Elizabeth Macpherson for her careful reading of the manuscript and her generous engagement with my work; Erin O'Donnell for reading the work in its early stages and offering sharp comments; Rafi Youatt for hosting me at the New School for Social Research for an important period in the book's development; Anne McNevin for excellent comments that honed a lot of the argument; Serge Gutwirth for his consistent support, encouragement, and keen observations; Alessia Tanas for engaging with so much of my work and introducing me to many parallels that I had not seen; Marcel Wissenburg for being a trusted intellectual companion and sounding board for half-baked ideas; Jakob Horstman, my editor at transcript, for bearing with the project and re-reading it too many times; the Research Foundation Flanders and the Vrije Universiteit Brussel's Political Science Department – without their financial support this work would have been impossible; the three anonymous reviewers that thoroughly and constructively engaged with the text.

My deep gratitude goes to the many scholars and practitioners that have pushed incessantly to change the dominant frameworks of legal theory and practice. Naming them exhaustively is impossible, but much of their work is present in this book. Established paradigms have outlived their usefulness, and the work of these courageous people is pushing these further into oblivion. My implicit or explicit critique of their work is undertaken in a spirit of deep solidarity, and towards the further concerted erosion of the status quo.

Chapter I: Introduction

Rights are ubiquitous in our world. In theory, if not always in practice, they belong to a growing number of subjects: humans have them, as well as inanimate objects (monuments and patrimonial goods), fictitious collective entities (corporations and states), and sometimes animals (usually the charismatic ones, though even then, not always). Rights provoke strong advocacy and inspire passionate struggle. Increasingly, for better or worse, they are seen to be an obligatory mechanism of emancipation. And lately, a new entity has come to be seen as a potential subject of rights: nature itself. Since the beginning of the 21st century, rivers, mountains, and whole landscapes have received rights and, with them, a new legal status.

The theory and practice of applying rights to nature usually goes by the catch-all phrase *the rights of nature*. This book is about them, and particularly about trying to understand where they come from and where they may lead. With the growing number of cases[1] of rights granted to nature comes a growing public awareness of this phenomenon, usually reflected in increasing media coverage of striking examples: the constitutional rights of nature in Ecuador, the Law of Mother Earth in Bolivia, the legal personality of Whanganui river in Aotearoa, New Zealand, or the rights of rivers in Colombia, India, and Bangladesh, to mention but a few.[2]

---

1 I will use case in the colloquial sense, not the technical one used in jurisprudence. Where I do use the technical term, the context should make it obvious.

2 Rights of nature proposals are currently being drafted in many different places, for example in Bangladesh, Mexico, Uganda, Australia, to name but

The underlying assumption is often that all of these cases are fundamentally similar – part of a nature rights movement – and that they are (at least in theory) a radical solution to environmental degradation.

But practice has not yet proven that these kinds of rights are a good mechanism of environmental protection. Instead, it has demonstrated that these rights are of various kinds, have appeared in different contexts, and embody tensions and contradictions that predate them. The variety of cases to date begs for critical examination, one that aims to understand these rights as dispassionately as possible. This is what this book tries to accomplish, by engaging in a critique of the theory and practice of rights for nature. This may also help their future.

The context within which a trend is placed matters greatly for how it may be understood. The rights of nature appear at a historical moment unlike any other, one where human and geological history become intertwined (Chakrabarty 2009). To be precise, they appear at the intersection of two events that are really part of a delicate unity: the intensification of human pressure on the environment and the expansion of liberalism in the guise of increasing numbers, and kinds, of rights. Crucially, this later expansion is largely inseparable from the concomitant history of colonialism and Indigenous[3] subjugation.

Let's start with the latter. Since at least the 18th century, European philosophy, political, and legal practice has undergone several massive shifts towards a human world conceived of essentially in terms of rights and obligations. This has become so dominant that it is hard to imagine just how revolutionary this has been. Indeed, the French and American revolutions are rightly seen as paradigmatic examples of human rights applied on the basis of membership in the human species alone, without any consideration of social

---

a few. In Europe, these are present in some form in Sweden, the UK, Spain, and the EU as such.

3 In line with widely accepted international norms, Indigenous People will be capitalized. When referring to indigeneity in any other way but specific people, 'indigenous' will be used, as in 'indigenous thought'.

class, gender, ethnicity, and so on. This, of course, was the theory. In practice, human rights have never been equally distributed and continue to be a highly unequal tool (Douzinas 2000).

Concomitantly with the rise of rights as not only a salient, but also an increasingly important, category, the Western world invented a mode of political economy defined by the perpetual expansion of capitalism. Political liberalism therefore became split between two mutually reinforcing poles: stressing the importance of individual rights and stressing the necessity for free movement of capital. The ideological explanation has been for quite some time that one is indispensable to the other. During the cold war the 'free world' made the argument that its freedom passed through both its upholding of individual rights and its economic liberalism. With the end of that bipolar world, in the early 1990s, the victory of liberalism was hastily announced. The proponent of the "end of history" thesis (Fukuyama 1989) has since changed his mind (to his great credit), but the ideology that unites individual rights with economic liberalism has endured.

I cannot do justice to this long and complex history, and that is not what I am setting out to do. Others have done a superb job already (among others, Charbonnier 2020, Malm 2016, Mitchell 2011). What I do want to point out is that the rights of nature are best understood in the context of this double movement of rights expansion and intensification of human pressure on the environment through capital flows. In *Carbon Democracy*, Timothy Mitchell shows how the exploitation of coal reserves and the creation of a workforce able to exploit it was inseparable from political revolutions that secured rights for workers (that were, because of the material properties of coal, in a position to interrupt capital flows). On the other hand, Andreas Malm demonstrates, in *Fossil Capital*, how the transition to fossil fuels was elaborately designed precisely in order to control labor and concentrate it in places and around schedules that suited capital accumulation and expansion. Later on, the availability of artificially cheap energy became inseparable from a series of social transformations, including the creation of consumer cultures able to absorb excess production.

The political economic transformation of the past centuries has been, ecologically speaking, a train wreck long in the making. Usually though, the story of capitalist expansion is told as a separate story from that of the liberal expansion of rights. It is more helpful to instead look at the connections, and one way to see them clearly is by exploring briefly the way in which the contemporary dominance of a globalized economy works on the basis of an increased number of rights, selectively applied. One of the ways to see this connection comes, perhaps surprisingly, from chemistry. In 2000, Paul Crutzen, a leading geochemist, and biologist Eugene Stoermer, proposed that the planet had entered a new geological era, one termed the Anthropocene. This would replace the Holocene, the era that corresponded with the mild climate that is usually credited to have been instrumental in the development of civilizations in the past 12000 years or so.

The Anthropocene, in geochemical terms, simply means that future geologists will be able to discern a layer of human-made materials at the top crust of the Earth. Therefore, they would be entitled to conclude that the boundary between Holocene layers and the new materials was the boundary between two different times, marked by different geological processes (Waters et al 2016). In other words, Crutzen and Stoermer suggested that human activity had become a form of geological activity in terms of its transformational potential, on par with volcanic eruptions and tectonic movements (also see Crutzen 2002, 2006, Zalasiewicz et al 2011). Officially, the geological community has not yet adopted the term as fact. This notwithstanding, it has had a tremendous influence, because it captures a qualitatively different time, not just a geologically different one.

Climate change is but the most visible, and most discussed, of Anthropocene problems. But it is not the only one. Biodiversity loss, land use changes, fresh-water use, the nitrogen cycle – all of these are equally important processes that have been formidably altered by human activity. Critical scholars have rightly pointed out that the idea of an Anthropocene focuses too much on 'humanity' having influenced 'the planet', when instead what is truer is that a select number of people, and the processes of accumulation that they have set in motion, have altered the planet for everyone. Jason Moore, for example, has therefore proposed the Capitalocene as an alternative name (Moore 2017, 2018). I have proposed the term Ecocene (Tănăsescu 2022) as an alternative that focuses on the political importance of ecological processes themselves. Beyond the terminological discussion, it is important to see that the era of human geological influence has come into being as both a radically unequal process (most CO2 emissions are highly concentrated in some places, for example), and on the basis of a culture of expanding rights.

Some of the scholars responsible for introducing the Anthropocene have also been very active in trying to understand when it began (Zalasiewicz et al 2016). There are several candidates, usually placed around the industrial revolution, though others have implied that the Holocene itself was always already the Anthropocene, as humans have modified environments for a long time indeed (Ellis et al 2021). The most useful and, in a sense, obvious date for the beginning of the new era is 1945. Two things are put in motion at that time that will come to be overly important for the ways in which the planet is modified. On the one hand, 1945 inaugurates the atomic era, with explosions and tests that have left a clear mark on the upper crust of the Earth. On the other hand, the end of World War II ushered in the era of the Great Acceleration: a time in history where a select number of societies (mostly Western, but increasingly not so) started producing and consuming stuff at an exponentially growing rate, all predicated on the availability of fossil energy.

Graphs showing the settling in of the Great Acceleration are striking: for a great number of things, there is a J shaped curve from the end of the second world war until today, both in terms of its production and consumption (energy, consumer goods, food stuff – particularly chicken, fertilizers, cement, plastics, and so on). During the same time though, the liberal heritage of rights, with foundations in earlier revolutions against monarchy, really came into its own. The period of the Great Acceleration is also the period of the Universal Declaration of Human Rights. But the exponential increase in churning Earth's stuff is not some natural process that humans cannot but obey. Instead, it has been a deliberate program of political economy that has managed to put together two seemingly disparate movements: one towards increasing exploitation of resources and labor (both in the form of increasing extraction of raw materials and of their processing for consumption) and one towards increasing human liberty.

This is the genius of the current system of globalized, intense exploitation: it doesn't merely tolerate the expansion of rights discourses; it uses it to its advantage, even though the indefinite production of stuff exemplified most strikingly in the doctrine of infinite economic growth cannot but exploit human resources as much as natural ones. The way in which this hegemonic system of production/consumption accomplishes this feat is through the power of the nation state to selectively apply rights in a way that matches with the interests of global capital expansion. This collusion between the *national* state and capitalist expansion is not a recent invention, but there from the beginning of nations themselves (Sharma 2020). Without it, much of the structure on which the Great Acceleration depends would collapse.

The fact that the correct (one may even say utopian) application of rights would be existentially threatening to global capitalism does not mean that rights are *the* tool of emancipation. In fact, their having become the go-to tool of emancipatory politics has so far helped capitalist expansion and the indefinite production that characterizes it. This is an argument that I will weave throughout the book. I wanted to start the discussion of rights for nature by setting it in an appropriate context, one where it is almost never set, partly because of the naïve belief that rights are a good in themselves.

*

This book has a simple goal: it aims to introduce the idea of rights for nature from a critical perspective. Recognizing that times of great uncertainty can elicit unwarranted enthusiasm for universal solutions, I cannot present the rights of nature as an inherent cure for contemporary and future problems. Instead, I opt to present it critically, which means that I want to spend some time understanding where this idea comes from, and what it can be applied to with reasonable expectations of success. I am also interested in thinking about what 'success' may mean, what it may look like in practice. In other words, this is not the book of a believer, though I like to think that it would be good for believers as well.

It will become clear throughout that the guiding question of this book – what the rights of nature mean – does not have a single answer. Instead, the argument will spend some time developing the multiple answers demanded by a critical perspective. It is not a matter of competing answers, as if one could find, if only enough effort were spent, the correct one. Instead, the rights of nature have both multiple histories and multiple meanings, all coexisting and mutually determining the continuing evolution of ideas and practices. It is this multiplicity that is most interesting, and the best route towards some level of understanding.

Fortunately, there are already enough cases of rights granted to nature to be able to present the multiplicity of theory and practice. Showcasing this multiplicity is not an end in itself, but has two very clear goals. On the one hand, it is meant to counter what I call "rights of nature orthodoxy", a view of these rights as inherently positive constructions (or, at worst, benign) that are going to save 'the environment' from rapacious 'humans'. I will show that this is at best an unfounded belief, and at worst an actively dangerous one. Its propagation risks derailing the evolution of rights for nature towards a diversity of views that can tackle a diversity of situations.

On the other hand, my goal is to empower practitioners, general readers, as well as future scholars by presenting some critical tools that can help in the necessarily long-term and patient work of building alternative ways of living (which will themselves be multiple). Critical scholarship has already provided a series of insights that remain mostly ignored by many advocates invested in defining a mainstream. My argument is not that rights for nature are unhelpful or dangerous, but rather that we need to be much more reflective in how and why they are used. In this, it helps to be clear about the different intellectual genealogies present in different cases, and how these influence outcomes irrespective of the desires of their proponents. It also helps to be clear as to why different versions of these rights may be deployed, and by who.

I think it's helpful to start by giving the conclusions away. At this point they may not convince, but that is not the idea behind presenting them up front. Rather, I wish to clearly delineate the structure of the critical engagement with the rights of nature, such that often-repeated tropes about them are exorcised before we begin. Together, the following propositions are indispensable for thinking about the rights of nature:

1. *The rights of nature are both theoretically and practically possible.* They make theoretical sense and, largely because of this, they have been adopted in different places. It is important to realize right away that the claim that rights cannot be predicated of nature is both theoretically and practically untrue; they can, they have, and they will continue to be predicated. It is pointless to argue that the rights of nature are nonsense.
2. *The rights of nature are not a monolith.* Despite the often-repeated claim that the rights of nature constitute a movement, there has been very little reflection on what the movement is made of, and what it means for the expansion of these rights to be thought of as a movement. In many cases, they have taken the form of an elite proposition in search of a grassroots, and not the other way around. Rights of nature legislations have appeared in different places and in radically different ways. There has been international diffusion of this idea, to be sure, but this does not mean that all cases can be subsumed under a unifying label propagated by a broad movement. The internal diversity of the idea, and of its practice, deserves being foregrounded, as it is a valuable asset going forward.
3. *The most useful frame for understanding the rights of nature is political, not legal.* One cannot understand what the rights of nature are *doing* without thinking about them in terms of power relations. All too often, strictly legal interpretations forget that legal norms are as good as their implementation, which necessarily passes through political power. This may be true in general, but in the particular case of rights for nature it is extremely important. Specifically, the question of who has the power to represent a nature with rights is central to understanding their potential.

This does not mean that local legal contexts do not matter; they matter greatly! But what ultimately gives the rights of nature practical purchase is the political process that leads up to them, and that makes or breaks their implementation.

4. *The rights of nature are not primarily about nature.* This may seem counterintuitive, but it follows from proposition 3 above. The rights of nature are neither a universal solution to environmental harm, nor uniquely placed to solve such harm. In fact, they are not primarily about the environment at all, but about creating new relations through which environmental concerns may be differently expressed. What 'environmental concerns' look like is entirely dependent on the power configuration that births them.
5. *How rights of nature laws/provisions/regulations are drafted matters a lot!* This follows from proposition 4. I will attend to some of the differences and variations in legal texts so far and show how these variations are not just legal minutiae but crucial for understanding. What on the face of it look like similar cases will end up, after attending to the details, to be wildly different. These differences matter.

Let us begin.

Chapter II: Rights Meet Nature
A Brief History

Origin stories are important. On the face of it, they reveal where something comes from. But that is not their main function; instead, they embed concepts and events within a narrative that gives them an overarching meaning, and therefore a particular direction. Origin stories manipulate how we view the thing under discussion, attempting thus to control how it may evolve.

The rights of nature are no exception to this. It makes sense to start their investigation with their history, but immediately a problem arises: which history? Is it the case that they only have one history, as more or less all commentators so far have implied? And if only one, which one? How can that be decided? Is a history synonymous with the *earliest* appearance of something, or with the form that most endures? These are questions that cannot be immediately answered. I raise them in order to begin this investigation grounded in the lucidity of the choices ahead. By recounting the history of rights for nature, I cannot claim to be recounting the only veridical history. Instead, I am necessarily selecting among predecessors in order to make a greater point.

Slowly, a standard history of rights of nature has become orthodoxy. I am well placed to know this particular history, as I have contributed to making it orthodoxy (Tănăsescu 2016). After recounting it, I want to turn to other versions that will inevitably complicate a simple origin story, adding to the layers that current theory and practice cannot but inherit. What I want to show is that they have multiple and competing histories, and what we choose to highlight has to be interpreted as a wider move of signification, and not simply as recounting the historical truth. After presenting multiple versions of their genesis, I will turn to the question of whether or not granting rights to nature was, in some sense, and despite all possible histories, inevitable. The chapter will therefore end with an investigation of the seemingly fateful collision of rights with nature.

Cristopher Stone and Legal Standing

The standard version of the history of rights of nature starts with the work of legal scholar Cristopher Stone. In a 1972 article titled Should Trees Have Standing? - Toward Legal Rights for Natural Objects (Stone 1972), Stone explicitly argued that the environment could enjoy legal rights.[1] He developed this line of thinking further in his 2010 book *Should Trees Have Standing? Law, Morality and the Environment*. Stone's arguments are still extremely influential, so it makes sense to pause and look at them closely.

What occasioned Stone's thinking was a lawsuit, brought by the Sierra Club.[2] In *Sierra Club v Morton*, "the U.S. Forest Service had granted a permit to Walt Disney Enterprises, Inc. to 'develop' Mineral King Valley, a wilderness area in California's Sierra Nevada Mountains, by the construction of a $35 million complex of motels, restaurants, and recreational facilities. The Sierra Club, maintaining that the project would adversely affect the area's aesthetic and ecological balance, brought suit for an injunction" (Stone 2010: xiii). However, the Ninth Circuit ruled that the Sierra Club did not have

---

1 Any claim to an "earliest" version of something – here, the rights of nature – should be treated with care. Chances are that, if one looks more closely, one finds predecessor that only vary by degree from the supposed origin of an idea. For example, Nash (1989, p.127) quotes a 1964 essay by Clarence Morris that specifically dealt with "nature's legal rights". Surely, there were predecessors for that as well! The point is that nothing can be settled by finding the earliest version; historical and intellectual threads are living and themselves respond to present tugging and wrangling.

2 One of the most influential environmental organizations in the Unites States of America. See https://www.sierraclub.org

legal standing to bring the suit. An appeal arrived in front of the Supreme Court, which ended up agreeing with the Ninth Circuit, though Justice Douglas penned a now famous dissent based on Stone's legal argumentation.

Stone's basic argument was simple: Sierra Club did not sue on behalf of Mineral King Valley because they were interested in protecting their own aesthetic interests; they were interested in protecting the integrity of the place itself! However, the US doctrine of legal standing did not allow them to sue because they could not show that they would be directly impacted by the proposed construction. There was no place in US law for suing on behalf of an environment *itself*, irrespective of damage to the person suing. To have standing, then, means to have the right to bring a lawsuit in front of a judge, because you are considered an injured party. Why not, then, allow standing to apply directly to the natural entities that the Sierra Club was trying to protect?[3]

Stone shows convincingly that organizations like the Sierra Club have had to retort to all sorts of subterfuges in order to gain legal standing (things like claiming 'aesthetic injury'). It would be much simpler if the law legitimized their motives to begin with, by granting standing to the natural entities themselves. The dissent that Justice Douglas wrote was based on Stone's paper and argued that "public concern for protecting nature's ecological equilibrium should lead to the conferral of standing upon environmental objects to sue for their own preservation" (quoted in Stone, 2010: xiv). In his work, Stone was careful to show that this is much less radical than it first appears. In fact, there are many non-human and even non-animate entities that do enjoy legal standing, for example ships and corporations. These last ones are of particular interest,

3 It is important to realize that the doctrine of standing is not the same everywhere. Stone was specifically reacting to the US version of standing, whereas in other jurisdictions – say, Finland or New Zealand – individuals or groups not directly affected can still sue on behalf of an environment, claiming that they are defending the common good or interest (Kurki 2019). This is an important contextual element in understanding the genesis of the standing argument in rights of nature advocacy.

and I will come back to them throughout the book. For now, it suffices to show that the particular history of rights of nature rooted in Stone's work starts with a concern for achieving legal standing. This concern makes sense for the legal system of the United States but is obviated by public interest environmental legal standing in other jurisdictions around the world.

There is no problem with conferring legal standing on anything at all. The only limiting factor, as it were, is what people empowered to confer such standing consider deserving of it, for pragmatic reasons. In order to make this case, it helps to show that having legal standing comes with the creation of a legal personality: whoever or whatever has legal standing becomes, because of that, a 'person' in front of the law. Legal personality and legal standing are a package; you cannot have one without the other.

According to several influential legal scholars (Naffine 2003, 2009, 2011 Grear 2013), legal personality is granted by the law in a highly fluid and malleable fashion. This means that a legal person is that entity that the law declares to be a legal person; it's that simple. The interesting question is *why* certain entities are deemed, by the law, to enjoy legal personality, and others are not. And that is precisely the terrain on which the rights of nature develop. Both in terms of advocacy and theory, rights of nature advocates have insisted for a long time that there are no valid apriori reasons to use the construct of legal personality for some entities, but not for nature.

For Stone, as well as for many of his followers, the question of legal standing for nature is intrinsically tied to its moral standing: nature should have legal standing because it is morally worthy of such. This argument is borrowed from the sister discourse of animal rights, where the moral status of an animal is deemed one of the most important features for determining its legal status. The conflation of legal and moral personality leads to the belief that the world is experiencing, to paraphrase Peter Singer (1973), a growing circle of moral concern.[4] In Stone's language, "there is something of

4 Peter Singer is the most visible contemporary advocate of this position, but the idea of an expanding circle of ethical concern is much older than his work,

a seamless web involved: there will be resistance to giving the thing 'rights' until it can be seen and valued for itself; yet, it is hard to see it and value it for itself until we can bring ourselves to give it 'rights' — which is almost inevitably going to sound inconceivable to a large group of people" (Stone 1972: 456).

This makes it seem as if moral and legal personality are related in a vectored fashion: if something has moral standing, then it is apt for getting legal standing; conversely, granting legal standing should soften the moral imagination of an increasing number of people. As comforting as this thought may be, it is not supported by legal practice, nor by the way in which moral considerations tend to work. This is not to say that some entities that are morally considerable do not receive legal status on that account. Nor is it to say that the law has no bearing on how morality develops. But it is to say that there is no automatic relationship between the two.

The easiest way to see this is to think about the countless entities that enjoy legal standing without also enjoying, on that account, moral standing. Retrieving the examples of ships and corporations, it seems clear that neither of these two enjoy moral standing just because they have the legal kind. Conversely, many cultures extend moral standing to ancestors and spirits, but without this translating into any kind of legal status akin to the Western concept of 'legal person'. The point is that, though the two kinds of standing are entangled within the rights of nature from the beginning of their history, this entanglement itself should be actively questioned rather than simply assumed. It is just not the case that extending legal rights to the environment is uniquely a response to this latter's moral standing, nor that it would automatically lead to moral improvement.

There will be ample opportunity later on to engage this point further. Now, I want to point out that in the history of rights of nature that starts with Stone, the main concern seems to be with the notion of legal standing, which is often interpreted to respond to a kind of moral status that the law has previously failed to recognize. But this association between legal and moral standing is neither

---

going back at least to the philosophy of Jeremy Bentham (one of the major influences on Singer's work).

central, nor unique, to Stone. In fact, his work is that of a pragmatist, interested in reaching towards whatever conceptual tools are at hand that may solve a perceived problem. Though Stone certainly speaks about legal and moral standing in analogous ways, he does not develop the connection to great length, nor does he seem – on my reading – to be primarily interested in it. Though the pragmatist orientation is pronounced in his work, this does not mean that it is equally pronounced in rights of nature scholarship more broadly, even that which claims Stone as a fundamental inspiration. In fact, the moral-legal standing equivocation that Stone inherits wholesale and neither questions nor makes central became a persistent strand within the history of the rights of nature, so much so that we find it, in much starker terms, if we switch the origin story altogether.

Godofredo Stutzin, Thomas Berry, and the Theology of Rights

Around the same time that Stone was writing his famous legal article, Godofredo Stutzin was putting the bases of environmental advocacy in Chile. The son of German immigrants, Stutzin was a lawyer with a deep and abiding love for all things natural. Writing in Spanish, his work travelled much less than that of Stone, simply because English became the dominant language of liberal ideology in the 20th century. But the fact remains that, as early as 1973,[5] Stutzin penned articles calling for the rights of nature. His arguments were like Stone's but also contained a different emphasis that continues to haunt[6] rights of nature theory and practice today.

It may be no surprise that the history of rights for nature in the Southern parts of the American continent is much more consciously influenced by Stutzin, though references to Stone still abound. A big

5 See Stutzin (1984) recounting the history of his own argumentation, as well as Simon (2019: 310).

6 Haunt because it is largely unconscious, as very few people actually cite Stutzin. For example, Stutzin's kind of rights of nature are very well exemplified by Boyd (2017), who doesn't cite him at all.

part of that influence is seen through the argument that these rights represent an ecocentric turn in the history of law. Stutzin himself saw them as responding to what he called an "ecological imperative". He argued that granting nature rights logically "implies overcoming the anthropocentric bias of law" (in Estupiñán Achury et al 2019: 41). This apparently simple formulation has had far-reaching consequences for the way in which rights of nature are understood, and therefore also for the way in which legal provisions are written. The implication of Stutzin's argument (a fundamental shift towards ecocentrism) is that it is through granting nature rights that environmental problems can be fixed.

"Every day it becomes more obvious", he wrote, "that if we want sustainable and long-lasting solutions to the ecological problems we have created, we cannot continue ignoring the existence of a nature with its own interests"[7] (Stutzin 1984: 97). This means that nature's rights are formulated as *recognized*, not invented or granted by humans. The role of the human here is not of creating a legal mechanism, but rather of using legal mechanisms to translate what is already the case. For Stutzin, as well as for his followers, the moral standing of nature obviously demands legal standing, the two being inseparable. Furthermore, once the law catches up with the supposedly obvious fact of nature's moral standing, ecological problems can be solved, *because of* this alignment of the law with moral sensibility. This belief is succinctly summarized in the subtitle of an influential book on the rights of nature (Boyd 2017): "a legal revolution that could save the world".

This general outline of advocacy and theory is a very durable and potent one. I would even argue that Stutzin's influence on the rights of nature, though much less acknowledged than Stone's, has so far been more potent. It has, to be sure, had a great influence on one of the first codifications of these rights, in Ecuador's 2008 constitution (see Chapter 3 for an extended discussion). Whereas for Stone granting rights to nature was mostly about the pragmatism of legal standing, for Stutzin it was about righting a wrong. The concept of right itself approaches here the older idea of natural right, that

7 Own translation.

is to say the correct form of something, and its correct treatment, as dictated by nature itself. Whereas for Stone legal standing pragmatically led to formatting nature as legal personality, for Stutzin it is the literal personality of nature that demands we recognize its rights (notice how, in the quote above, Stutzin refers to nature's *interests*).

The idea of legal personality, as I have argued above, goes together with that of standing, but it also brings its own flavor to the discussion. Stutzin's insistence on the imbrication of legal and moral standing accomplishes a similar imbrication of legal and moral personality. The legal person, in strictly legal terms, is a fiction that can be granted to many kinds of entities inasmuch as the law deems it necessary (O'Donnell 2021, Naffine 2017). But the very terms legal *person* or *personality* already point towards the moral traces that are etched within this legal concept (Grear 2013, Naffine 2003, 2011). Stutzin doesn't speak of the possibility of formatting nature as a legal *entity*, but rather of the – to him – obvious personal qualities of nature that demand a recognition of its rights.[8]

The kind of argumentation that Stutzin employs found many hires, not least in a spiritualist tradition that theologizes the recognition of nature's inherent value through the concept of rights. The most influential early proponent of a specifically *ecotheological* take on nature's potential rights was Thomas Berry, though he was himself building on a long tradition that theologized the idea of rights, rooted in the concept of natural right. In his turn, Berry decisively influenced the work of Cormac Cullinan, which became – through his book *Wild Law* (2011) – an important foundation for rights of nature scholarship and practice. Thomas Berry was a cultural historian and theologian that focused much of his work on the idea

---

8 In legal theory, there is another salient distinction between legal *subject* and legal person, with the subject encompassing, potentially, a more agnostic view of the entity thus created. For the purposes of this book, I will use legal person, as I think it reflects better its use in rights of nature so far, and contrast it with legal entity, which is also supported by some extant cases. See Tănăsescu (2020).

that the way in which the world is narrated by different cultures is changing, and he wanted to participate creatively in this change by offering a new kind of story.

The story that Berry advanced is best exemplified by the title of his last book, *The Great Work* (2011). This, the culmination of his activity, reunited ideas that he had presented throughout a series of earlier publications as well as teaching and public engagement. For my purposes here, several elements of Berry's account of the Universe are relevant, especially inasmuch as they cut a channel for the rights of nature to travel through that becomes increasingly moralist.

The first thing that deserves pointing out is that Berry's story is a grand narrative of *the Universe*. His interest in grand narratives follows directly from theology, which is quite obviously interested in the greatest possible level of explanation for observable phenomena.[9] Wishing to reconcile Christian theology with modern science, particularly cosmology and ecology, he focused on a grand narrative that explained the way in which the Universe – the greatest possible unit – came into being and evolved. To his credit, Berry took on board scientific theories, like evolution, and worked theology around them, rather than the other way around (just like his great influence, Teilhard de Chardin). So, instead of a theological universe that arranged things according to God's plan, Berry argued for an evolutionary universe created by God precisely so as to be self-generating (also see Robinson 1991).

The focus on the great totality was broken down through what Berry called the twelve principles. It is beyond my scope to go through all of them, but some are extremely useful for getting across an accurate picture of the kind of conceptions that, through Berry and Cullinan, made their way into the rights of nature. The most important aspect to discuss is succinctly summed up in

9 To be fair, there are theological interpretations of ecology that do not focus on the great totality. For example, Berry's namesake, Wendell Berry, has focused much of his impressive body of work on the specificity of place, rather than the planetary whole, though he is also decidedly Christian in his approach.

Berry's second principle, namely that the universe is a unity. This principle of unity is a way of reconciling the theological unity of creation (one creator and one creation) with the interrelatedness that ecology had been uncovering since its 19th century beginnings. The fact of interrelatedness is made to sit comfortably within the theological idea of unity by interpreting the universe as a vast community. The argument is that, given that everything is related to everything else, everything must be a participant in the great community of being (in the Great Work).

However, this is not some form of post-humanism, a radically egalitarian distribution of agency among beings (a la Bruno Latour). Because of human's privileged role within creation, it is only through human consciousness that the great community the universe is thought to be, comes to know itself. This places humans in a responsible position, as *guardians* of the great mystery. The amalgamation of the ideas of unity and community, together with the privileging of human consciousness, leads towards a picture of the world that is both hierarchical (in the theological tradition of the Great Chain of Being; see Descola 2013, 2014) and, by its own account, ecocentric. Berry complains that previous law had been anthropocentric, only valuing nature inasmuch as it served human needs. He therefore proposes ecocentric conceptions, that is, ones that would value nature for its own sake. But the theological underpinnings of his argument render the whole ecocentric – anthropocentric distinction meaningless, as it is ultimately the responsibility of humans to uphold the order of creation by refashioning their law to fit with the interrelatedness of a universal community.

The conception of ecology that Berry's work is based on is that of the early 20th century, where the greatest figure was Eugene Odum, who significantly advanced the idea of ecosystem coined by Arthur Tansley. Already in the 1970s though, precisely when Berry started his work, Odum's ecosystem ecology came under sustained attack, first in the work of Drury and Nisbet (1973), who argued that the ecosystem is a sociological import into ecology, mimicking the sociological idea of community but without a factual basis in what ecologists observed. For Drury and Nisbet, there was no such thing as a 'natural community', except as a fiction of the sociologically (or theologically, as Berry shows) biased mind. What the ecologist observed was an endless series of variations and interactions among animals and plants, with alliances in constant flux (Drury 1998). The critique of the ecosystem concept has been very influential, in ecology, but much less so in popular understandings of this science, which continue to use the concept as if it corresponded to some naturally ordained state of things.

Berry's idea of community mimics the idea of an ecosystem in early 20th century ecology. It is an interpretation of the fact of interrelation that selectively picks ecological concepts such that they can cohere with theological commitments. But this leaves Berry's concepts condemned to a level of abstraction that cannot differentiate between genuinely different situations. If all is unity and totality, then it is only at the greatest level of analysis that law, for example, can intervene. And this is precisely how his work has been made useful for law by Cormac Cullinan.

In *Wild Law*, Cullinan extracts from Berry several different nature rights that he argues are the fundamental ones – derived, as it were, from Berry's ontology (or rather, theology). These are the right to exist, to have a habitat, and to evolve as part of the earth community. The parallels with human rights discourse are striking. Recall, for example, that Thomas Jefferson's fundamental rights were to life, liberty, and the pursuit of happiness (also see discussion of Nash below). For a legal orientation that claims to be ecocentric, the kinds of rights proposed seem to be direct imports from anthropocentric conceptions. I will explore this point in more detail below. What I want to point out here is that Cullinan's rights, as direct hires of Berry's theology, are predicated at the level of the totality and presuppose the existence of such a thing as an Earth Community. This thinking has had a profound influence on several cases of rights for nature so far. But practice has also been more diverse than theory and therefore has offered ways of thinking about rights that do not have to be grounded in ecotheology (see Chapter 4). It is only through the kind of political framework that I am proposing here that we can even see the difference.

The history of the rights of nature that goes from Stutzin to Berry to Cullinan is one that is quite different from the most popular version of these rights as emanating from Stone's work. Stone was first and foremost a pragmatist, and his work does not give much sustained attention to the concept of nature as totality as opposed to locality, or to the kinds of things that standing could apply to. For Stone, standing can apply to anything, and if a great number of people find it necessary to speak on behalf of environments, the law can accommodate that.[10] However, the ecotheological history that I have briefly sketched doesn't seem to be primarily interested in the pragmatism of given situations, but rather in advancing a framework that subsumes any given situation under the Great Work, the totality that imposes, as if on its own, a series of 'fundamental rights' that have to be *recognized* (as opposed to granted). Cullinan uses the expression Great Jurisprudence to describe his framework, in an obvious reference to Berry.[11] This way of thinking is moralistic because it implies that anyone that does not share the fundamentally theological assumptions underlining it is not only wrong, but fails to grasp a universal *moral* truth.

In another relatively early work on the concept of rights for nature (*The Rights of Nature. A History of Environmental Ethics*, 1989), Roderick Nash analyzed how the idea of rights for nature emerged in the English-speaking world out of the earlier conceptions of natural right that were successively modified through the human rights revolutions (abolitionism and women's rights first and foremost), theories of animal rights, and eventually the rights of nature itself. What is extremely interesting for my purposes here is how Nash, though himself subscribing to an 'expanding circle of moral concern' view, nonetheless shows the fine webbing that holds together apparently disparate thinkers and traditions around the idea that rights are a *recognition* of something that is already there, and that this recognition can be expanded without limits (to eventually encompass everything).

10 In many jurisdictions it already does, without appealing to legal personality or rights at all (see Kurki 2019).

11 It may be worth pointing out that theological thinking does not present itself as a framework, but rather as a revelation of the truth (which leads to recognized, not granted, rights).

Nash also shows how theology was never far away from the earliest environmental concerns, nor from the very influential debate about the inherent value of nature. The passage from the 19th to the 20th century was a particularly fruitful period for the merging of ecology with value theories and theology. John Muir, for example, the mythical father of US national parks, was explicit in deriving the values that he saw as inhering in the natural world from the 'fact' of creation. The same Muir was a founding member of the Sierra Club that would eventually animate Stone's thinking. The particular history of the development of environmental ethics that Nash recounts draws on a variety of sources and inspirations (not only theology, to be sure), but stays firmly within dualistic conceptions of the universe. Even the idea of ecocentrism, reflected through movements such as deep ecology and often claimed by rights of nature theory and practice, does nothing to challenge binary thinking: the 'center' is simply moved from one entity (the human) to another (nature). This obsession with centrism[12] is indeed a feature of much Anglo-American environmental ethics, and one decidedly important for the rights of nature.

There will be more opportunities to parse through the various consequences of this strand of rights, as well as ponder the possibility of de-moralizing the rights of nature so as to allow for a diversity of views to take hold. But before we get there, I want to focus a bit more closely on several other elements of this history that are extremely important. First and foremost, I need to attend to the concept of nature itself.

12 Not all environmental ethics and philosophy develops in this centric-biased way. For example, much French literature on these topics shies away from centrism. See Serres (1995), Latour (2004), Descola (2013), to mention but the most influential ones. Even more importantly, many philosophies labelled as 'indigenous' offer much richer conceptual tapestries through which to relate to the environment. One of the more important questions of this book is to what extent the concept of rights *forces* one towards the centrism of Anglo-American thought, and therefore away from relational thinking and surprising legal possibilities. For an excellent argument for relationality in law, see Macpherson (2021). Also see Tănăsescu (2021).

The Concept of Nature

The concept of nature is a baffling one, being simultaneously obvious and incredibly elusive. The obviousness comes solely from within a particular modern tradition of philosophizing that relegates nature to everything that is not culture. Perhaps the most succinct and coherent concept of nature within that tradition comes from Marxism, where nature is simply that which labor encounters (and which, therefore, it does not itself make; again, the background of human 'cultural' activity; Wark 2015). The elusiveness arises as soon as one thinks further about the distinction nature/culture, and realizes that there is no exact border to be found, but rather porosity all the way through. Anthropology compounds the problem further, having decisively shown that 'nature' is a culturally specific concept, and not at all the universal that modernity wants it to be (Descola 2013, De Castro 1996, 2014, 2019, Skafish 2016a, De la Cadena 2015, de la Bellacasa 2017).

The debate on the meaning of nature is important and vast, and I cannot survey it adequately or contribute to it in any meaningful way. But I do want to point out the cultural rootedness of the concept of nature. Second, I want to show that, based on the history sketched out so far, there are two very different ideas of nature at play within the rights of nature. Let us see what these are and the importance of their difference.

Godofredo Stutzin, in the 1984 version of his article, refers to Stone's minimalist conception of the rights of nature as dealing only with standing, but adds that in principle this can be applied to nature as such. We saw that in the work of Berry and his followers, we are always speaking about Nature (capital N), that is to say the totality, everything there is, and so on. According to Berry, this kind of Nature would not be modern at all, because it is not conceived of as mere background to human activity, which would be qualitatively different. Instead, Nature is *the* all-encompassing itself, and therefore human activity is definitionally natural. This poses a problem that is unresolved in this strand of rights for nature, namely the simultaneous use of the concept of nature as both a logical background and a kind of proxy for the good. This surreptitious moral use had already been anticipated by John Stuart Mill, whose essay *On Nature* demonstrates the incoherence of using the idea of nature as a proxy for the good.

Very briefly, Mill argues that the word nature is used to mean both what is so by its own design (and therefore is necessarily so), and what is *properly* so, therefore shifting into a moral register. However, there is no logical connection between the two. If anything, there is an inherent contradiction in using nature as both that which is so and that which *should* be so. In other words, the meaning of the word nature shifts when going from ontology (what is) to morals (what should be). On an even more basic level, Mill argues that if something is so by nature, it needs no encouragement to be so; conversely, if something is not so by nature, it needs no prohibition. In Tănăsescu (2016), I argued that Mill's argument (also see Antony 2000) implies that the supposed inherence of rights in the subject of rights (whether humans or 'nature') can be of no ethical significance. In other words, saying that rights are recognized confuses the ethical significance of rights (as proclamations) with the idea of an already moral nature. In fact, if rights were already part of nature, they would need no recognizing, just like the laws of physics operate whether they are recognized or not.

Mill's argument is, in my view, still very important to recall. But it's also worth pointing out that Nature conceived of as Totality is also hopelessly large, in such a way as to not admit of relationships that are situated at lower levels of abstraction. This is why, when Berry and his followers speak about Nature they also speak about the disturbing relationship that Humanity has had with it. Entertaining the idea that there might be such a thing as a relationship between two categories this big is an artefact of the concept of nature as Totality. No single individual, or particularly situated group (whether human or non-human) can ever enter into relationship with Nature but only, it would seem, with particular parts of its manifestations. This reliance on totality is extremely important to recognize, because it is one of the main bridges between rights of Nature and the neoliberal expansion of a particular model of development predicated on the existence of a universal Human with universal rights (also see Chapter 6). In actual fact, the human that stands for Humanity is consistently of particular socio-economic backgrounds inextricably linked with a removal from actual environments that is the modern abstraction par excellence.

Continuing the earlier parallel with the concept of ecosystem, here we see how any particular environment is immediately formatted as derivative, as somehow subservient to the Great Totality that gives it the laws of its functioning (which, as I've already pointed out, both include and exclude humans, in an incoherent way). It would be as if, in ecology, the ecosystem concept would have led to speaking of the Ecosystem as the ultimate reality, and any particular ecosystem simply as a reflection of it. This is in fact what happened to much Odum-inspired ecology, as it postulated a natural equilibrium that natural communities supposedly tended towards, something that is yet to be observed as a verifiable and stable fact of nature.

The science of ecology has moved from a mid-century preoccupation with balance to a current focus on "disturbance" as the normal state of nature, a concept that is much better suited to an era of anthropogenic changes than the idea of an inherent equilibrium. However, the theoretical rights of nature strand I am exploring here has consistently latched onto the earlier ecological science, translating its idea of balance into a norm of harmony (Kotzé and Calzadilla 2017, Calzadilla and Kotzé 2018): inasmuch as Nature is understood to be in some form of (now disturbed) balance, then the appropriate answer is to strive towards harmony between Humans and Nature (achievable through recognizing its rights).

Just like with the doctrine of human rights, which postulates a universal Human (see Douzinas 2000) as a general repository of fundamental rights, so this particular strand of rights postulates Nature as the origin of a set of fundamental rights, which must be extremely general. On the other hand, we can also think about a concept of nature as immediate environment, what David Abram talks about as an 'environing world' (Abram 2012; also see Tănăsescu 2022). This nature is very specific and highly textured, and it also changes through time without necessarily being derivative of a greater work. Māori, for example, perceive "the universe as a Process" (Kawharu 2010, 225). Nature as place, in other words, cannot admit of totalizing concepts but is instead focused on understanding how life is possible *here*, in this locality, under these changing conditions, with these participants. Nature as totality has no politics, only theology; nature as place is nothing but politics. Not incidentally, nature as place is also extremely well formulated in various indigenous philosophies[13] (for example, see Watts 2013), a point that I will come back to throughout.[14]

In the theoretical history of the rights of nature, Totality rules. However, in practice, nature as place has come to leave its mark within what its rights may mean. These issues are best explored through practical examples of rights for nature (see next chapter). Now, I want to attend to one last element that needs a bit of attention before moving on: the concept of rights.

---

13 Usually, indigenous systems of thought are variously referred to as 'beliefs', 'cosmovisions', 'cultures', and so on. This is done even by people, and legal texts, that are very inclusive. I find this terminology to be inadequate, because if draws a sharp line between what *we* have – proper systematic thinking, and what *they* have – beliefs and visions. José Gregorio Diaz Mirabal, coordinator of the Congress of Indigenous Organizations of the Amazon Basin (COICA), was quoted by Politico to have said, apropos international conventions, that Indigenous People are invited "to present our traditions, songs and dances". This is certainly not what communities around the world want; there is plenty of multicultural sensibility already. Instead of repeating the dominant terminology, I will refer to Indigenous thinking as either that – thinking, or as philosophy, the highest form of thought of 'our' culture. I see no reason why systematic thinking everywhere and anywhere should not be recognized as philosophy.

14 Interestingly, O'Donnell (2018) shows how law itself formats the idea of nature in different ways, but which all go substantially towards great levels of generality and, in part, reproduce dualisms. Nature is repeatedly understood by law as either the background of human activity, or as a thing to be protected, or – as is the case in the present discussion – as a legal person. But in all these instances the textures of places are absent, as are the relations that these textures inspire and sustain.

The Concepts of Rights and Legal Personality

The idea of granting rights to nature cannot be properly examined unless we also take stock of the concept of rights. As with nature before, I cannot possibly present a comprehensive overview of this concept, one of the most important ones in the Western philosophical cannon. However, besides pointing readers to masterful treatments of the subject, I want to simply pause and take stock of several different elements of rights that are crucial for this examination.

What, at its most basic, is a right? Following Wesley Newcomb Hohfeld (1917), still the most influential legal theorist on the matter, a right is a kind of enforceable claim. To what? That depends on the right, but basically to something that is owed to the rights holder, as a matter of justice. This is what Hohfeld calls claim-rights, and indeed the rights of nature are of this kind. Rights, under this account, are always correlated with duties, but the duty and the right need not coincide in the same holder. So, if a non-human holds a right, the correlative duty is on the human to treat the right-holding non-human in a particular kind of way. The possessor of such rights has a verifiable claim to be owed something, and therefore someone else has a duty in respect to the rights holder.

In *Environment, Political Representation, and the Challenge of Rights*, I developed in much more detail the relationship between rights and claims. There, I argued that what we think is owed to some entity is reflected in the kinds of rights that legal processes confer upon them. The mediation between the general form of a universal subject of rights and the specific rights conferred is accomplished through the idea of legal personality, which is a legal fiction that bridges universality and concreteness (2016, p.60). However, the idea of legal personality has both moral and legal components that, as I have already intimated, are often mixed together. Morally speaking, a legal person is a subject; legally speaking, a legal person is a place holder for the capacity to enforce rights. As Hartney put it, "whatever legal authorities say is a legal right, is a legal right, whether this agrees with what philosophers would say about moral rights" (in Tănăsescu 2016).

It is no surprise then that legal rights and legal personality go together. Kurki (2019) demonstrates that the legal person is defined by jurists as the holder of legal rights. He himself disagrees with this, what he calls the orthodox view of legal personality, but the point remains that in both legal theory and practice, rights and legal personality most often travel together. They certainly do in rights of nature theory and practice, as I will show in detail when discussing the cases of Ecuador and New Zealand (see Chapters 3 and 4).

Though having enforceable claims recognized by a legal authority seems to be, strictly speaking, a matter of legal proclamation, what philosophers have to say about who or what deserves rights is still of interest.[15] In legal philosophy, there have been two dominant (and competing) ways of accounting for why something may be eligible for rights. One way of accounting has been through "will theories", that is to say theories that demand the possession of full autonomy in order to be eligible for rights. The paradigmatic case here is a mature adult human in full possession of his capacities (the maleness of this paradigmatic figure has gone unquestioned for centuries). The most philosophically influential will theory is Immanuel Kant's attribution of full personhood to those capable of rationally setting their own moral law (see Kurki 2019, p.22). This basically eliminates most, if not all, non-humans from rights. In its most extreme versions, it also eliminates humans that, for some reason or another, are not considered fully rational.

Another basis for assigning rights and legal personhood has been explored by "interest theories". These do not focus on the capacity for autonomous decision but rather on the idea of interest, namely on whether the entity in question can have its own interests. This kind of thinking has been greatly influenced by Jeremy Bentham, the father of moral utilitarianism, who famously said vis-à-vis the moral consideration of animals that the question is not whether they can reason, but whether they can suffer. Interest theories therefore rely on stretching inherited conceptions

15 I cannot possibly do justice here to a long and important debate. The interested reader should especially consult Kurki's work on legal personhood, as well as Campbell (2011).

of interest, which can now be made to apply, in principle, to many different things (from ecosystems to corporations)

The relevant will versus interest debates are interesting in and of themselves, but for the purposes of rights for nature it suffices to simply point out that nature as such does not seem to fit easily within either way of arguing for rights, and therefore borrows liberally from both. Place-based nature may fare better, though advocates also argue that landscapes, for example, are sentient and have interests or exhibit self-determination. Whether rights advocates acknowledge the pedigree of their preferred concept or not makes little difference because these kinds of debates are baked into the concept of rights and accompany it no matter what. It stands to reason then that advocates would use any portrayal of nature that may fit will or interest theories of rights. And this is exactly what happened.

Already in the 1970s, when the contemporary rights of nature idea started its multiple paths, the Earth was starting to be thought of, within Western philosophy and science, as a vast organism. The most famous elaboration of this is James Lovelock's concept of Gaia, which simply states that the planet we inhabit is a self-regulating organism. Whatever Lovelock himself meant is one thing.[16] Quite another is the way in which the figure of Gaia was immediately appropriated by the rights of nature to mean that the Earth is *one living totality*, which precisely accords both with the history of liberal rights and with the theological strand that I briefly described earlier. All of a sudden, it seemed as if science itself was lending a helping hand by characterizing the planet in organismic terms that accorded with liberal rights.

With the figure of Gaia, the supposed expanding circle of moral concern seems to have come to its logical end. Moral theorists had argued for centuries that humanity has progressively expanded its moral circle by including more and more kinds of beings. The usual

---

16 The concept of Gaia is much more interesting than most of its popular appropriations so far. For one of the best discussions of Lovelock's idea, see Bruno Latour's *Facing Gaia* (2017). For a contemporary development of the concept of Gaia that is decidedly anti-theological, see Stengers (2015).

story starts with an image of humans only being concerned with their immediate family, then with the tribe, the village, the clan, and so on up to, now, the Earth. Whether law drives morality, or the other way around, has never really been decided: does law follow mores, or mores follow laws? Both have been argued by radical rights proponents (from Locke to Bentham to Salt and on to contemporary rights of nature and animal rights advocates – Peter Singer and Tom Reagan the most famous of them). The idea is not to settle, once and for all, on the correct causation. Rather, it is important to keep in mind the constitutive ambiguity of moral and legal conceptions of right and their reliance on a moral evolutionism that is part and parcel of important rights of nature strands today.

This moral evolutionism has also meant that radical advocates of rights expansions have drawn stark parallels between every level of the supposed expansion of concern. All rights struggles are supposed to be part of the same great circle, so women's rights, abolitionism, animal rights and now the rights of nature are all part of the same story, made to cohere by the idea of moral evolution itself, which relies on a stark distinction between thing (and therefore rightless) and subject (and therefore worthy of rights). Rights expansion would therefore be the passage of more and more things into subjects. So, the argument goes, slaves were things before the moral law made them persons, just like nature is a resource unless the moral law makes it a moral/legal person.[17]

From within a liberal tradition, the kind of moral evolutionary story sketched above seems almost obvious. However, there is not much evidence for it. The idea that narrow-circle humans only cared about their immediate family parallels Hobbes' idea of the state of nature, both of which are based on figments of imagination that are necessary for the idea of moral progress to function at all. Anthropology, for instance, has not unproblematically shown that the circle of concern starts small. If anything, the opposite might be

17 This argument is not particularly popular with minority rights activists, that see in it traces of their animalization, often used to deny them rights. Also see Tănăsescu (2016) for a detailed discussion of the thing/property versus person/subject distinction.

true: many a-modern societies predicate the moral universe on relations with the environing world *before* even those with their own family. We will see examples of this when we discuss Māori philosophies that are crucial for understanding the legal arrangements for nature in New Zealand. The point I want to make now is that the history of rights for nature as part of a rights expansion has no basis in empirical study, but is itself an inheritance of a way of arguing about morality and the law that is quintessentially Western and quintessentially part of a liberal tradition.

This does not mean that Indigenous Peoples, for example, have had nothing to do with different instances of rights for nature.[18] But exactly how indigenous philosophies interact with rights for nature is a matter for careful analysis, precisely so as to safeguard the radical potential of such philosophies against the hegemonic drive that rights are steeped in. This is extremely important, which is why it will feature throughout the rest of the argument. I now turn to setting the basis for further analyzing the indigenous relation to rights, both in general and specifically for nature.

Liberal Rights and Indigenous Histories

As may have become clear by now, rights for nature only superficially challenge the liberal history of rights. They are not only continuous with this history, but rather can only be properly understood by placing them within the liberal milieu of rights extensions. As Roderick Nash showed (1989), the rights of nature are understood by their proponents to be part and parcel of the rights revolutions that have decisively altered how we understand radical politics today. Campbell (2011) argued, not without reason, that contemporary political struggles are only taken seriously if they are couched in the language of rights. This itself attests to the power that rights discourses wield over the political imagination.

Miriam Tola (2018, 34) makes the same point by relying on the work of Gayatri Spivak (1999), where she argues that "rights are that

---

18 See O'Donnell et al (2020) for a careful discussion of multiple kinds of involvement.

which we cannot not want". However, she also points out that this instrument that cannot be unwanted also comes with an extensive state apparatus that it relies on for enforcement, and therefore with a certain way of understanding the relationship between the subject of rights and the state that grants them. In the case of the Ecuadorian constitution (see Chapter 3) this is as clear as can be, as we are dealing with a document so enamored with rights that it recognizes a plethora of them, impossible to uphold simultaneously, but together working to entrench the ultimately arbitrary power of the state (also see Tănăsescu 2016).

What I have called the moral evolutionism of liberal rights has also been theorized in terms of the existence of different rights generations. Karel Vasak (1984) proposed that the first-generation human rights has had to do with political and civil claims. The second targeted economic, social, and cultural rights; while the third has been termed by Morgan-Foster (2005) solidarity rights and encompasses everything that did not fit in the first two generations. Many critical scholars (see for example Douzinas 2000) have pointed out how the expansion of human rights discourses has chocked out other ways of conceiving of radical emancipation while being quite easily incorporated within liberal and capitalist status quos. Largely because of the association between liberalism and economic neoliberalism in the second part of the 20th century (and therefore the relentless pursuit of a particular kind of "development"), rights discourses have flourished, as neoliberal regimes have learned to both accept them and thrive on their infringement (also see Tzouvala 2020).

Slavery is a good example. Though it is no longer legal anywhere, in absolute numbers there have never been more people toiling under conditions of slavery than today (Bales et al 2009). It may seem paradoxical that in an era defined by the expansion of human rights, slavery would flourish. But it does so not just despite human rights, but also in part because all claims for emancipation are forced through rights language, which poses no fundamental challenges to the mechanisms generating a need for slave labor to begin with. Instead of an expanding circle of moral concern, we instead can witness a shifting pattern of exploitation. It is not the case that more and more people – to stick with human rights for the moment – have and enjoy full rights; it instead seems to be the case that the geography of rights and rightlessness shifts according to the needs of the global market. Rightlessness accompanies the search for ever-cheaper labor, while rightfulness extends to more and more domains of life that de facto require the perpetuation of conditions of domination (for example, things like consumer rights).

In the specific case of the rights of nature, scholars have already started to point out how they further legitimize rights discourses without any guarantee that this will actually translate into more substantive human or nature rights. Rawson and Mansfield (2018), for example, cunningly reverse the expression rights of nature in proposing that they in fact accomplish the *naturalization of rights*. It is as if the expanding circle narrative that is so central to the morality of non-human rights has become a self-fulfilling prophecy, where all efforts are put into expanding this one way of understanding relations (as claims) to every possible kind of subject. And it is on account of the expansion of moral claims to nature as such that a tenuous connection between rights for nature and indigenous philosophies is so often claimed.

It has become commonplace to present the rights of nature as either directly emanating from, or else closely approximating, indigenous philosophical and legal traditions. There is nothing within the various histories that I have so far surveyed that would warrant this claim. Why, then, is it so often made? There are, as I see it, three possible explanations: ignorance of indigenous philosophies, an unreflexive colonial inheritance, and enthusiastic belief in the power of rights discourse. These three reasons are mutually reinforcing: a superficial engagement with indigenous thought is already made possible by the still-influential inheritance of colonial ways of understanding indigeneity, and the omnipresence of rights discourses in modernity helps to further assimilate indigenous philosophies to Western ones. Nandita Sharma (2020) shows in detail how the colonial history that straddles the passage from imperial power to nation building has used rights *against* colonized populations.[19] This does not simply mean that rights were withheld, but quite the opposite: rights were used to divide and conquer and to cement an enduring association between indigeneity and living close to nature.

For example, she shows how many colonial powers took it upon themselves to protect Indigenous populations by granting selective rights to particular lands, fundamentally because colonists thought of Indigenous Peoples as "people of the land". In contrast, the category of "migrant" worked to displace people and throw them within global labor fluxes that appropriated their work while denying them the ability to belong to any place (they were not Indigenous). It is striking just how much this history endures today, when we still make stark distinctions between native people, understood to belong *by nature* to a particular place, and migrants who are essentially rightless precisely because of their being thought of as unplaceable. These kinds of distinctions between rightful belonging to a place and rightless migration have always underlined colonial enterprise and have crucially outlived it in post-colonial nations as well. Modern nation sates have continued to play a fundamental role in the definition of indigeneity as somehow related to the quest for rights (Niezen 2003, 11-12). The possibility of multiple belonging, or of relating to the land outside of the institution of ownership, or of welcoming strangers as kin, are all gone. The irony is that many of these possibilities are closer to indigenous philosophies than rights can ever be.

As I have argued previously, the concept of Nature as totality is often used as a bridge between the rights of nature and Indigenous People. But that kind of concept of nature has nothing indigenous about it. In fact, indigenous philosophies are routinely steeped within very particular environments that people relate to in genealogical ways. This is to say that many indigenous philosophies, though there are of course many differences between them, think

19 The same has been shown for the sister concept of legal personality, which was selectively used to punish slaves for their actions while denying their autonomy. See Bourke (2011).

about people as being derivative of specific places that are alive in ways that *are not analogous to personhood*. Vanessa Watts (2013) calls this "Place-Thought", that is to say a system of organizing life that is not separable from the particular place of its thinking.[20] Nature (or Earth) as Mother, the cliché often attributed to indigenous thought, is nothing but the obsession with totality dressed up as indigeneity.[21] Nature as totality is featureless and abstract, the exact opposite of place-thought.

This point is supported by a vast amount of literature by and on indigenous philosophies. To take another prominent example: Marisol de la Cadena, in her book *Earth Beings* (2015), patiently develops the intimate relationship between particular places and particular communities, while pointing out consistently how these relationships are not at all analogous to Humanity – Nature relations, nor are they reliant on an idea of personhood at all. What she calls Earth Beings are not approximations of Mother Earth, but kinds of creatures that act in *their* specific way and which enter into very precise relationships with surrounding communities (which, themselves, are not mere collections of individuals). In other words, there is a vast repository of living knowledge about different ways of inhabiting lands that shares little of the fundamental assumptions of liberal modernity.

It must be extremely frustrating for Indigenous thinkers and activists to constantly see their work appropriated in Western context in fundamentally the same way. As Indigenous thinkers, writers,

---

20 If we manage to stop thinking about indigeneity in ethnic terms (the inheritance of colonialism), and instead think about it as the cultivation of a certain kind of relationship with the land, we also start seeing, in the very centers of colonial modernity, strands of thinking that are particularly careful to emplacement. Wendell Berry, for example, directly acknowledges, in strikingly 'indigenous' tones, his thinking as being occasioned by his particular places, and therefore not being universal or total.

21 I do not mean to say that there is no conceptualization of nature as mother in Indigenous philosophies. For example, the Māori concept of Papatuánuku is explicitly feminine.

and critical anthropologists have shown repeatedly, there is a veritable well of radical political and legal conceptions available in a-modern contexts. Yet the only way in which Western philosophers and activists seem to be able to take stock of it is by positing personhood for Nature and reading rights into it! The pragmatic (though surely, on a personal level, often unintentional) reason for this is, as I have argued above, that personhood and rights are not fundamentally threatening to dominant modes of organizing social, political, and economic life. Thinking genealogically with landscapes that make the person look insignificant – now that is something truly revolutionary.

If we consider the tremendous momentum of the rights revolutions that have accompanied the growth of liberalism until today, it may seem almost inevitable that, eventually, rights would be predicated of nature. But inevitability does not mean predestination. What I want to draw attention to is the power of a discourse to cannibalize competing ones and to accommodate itself within wider power struggles. The consumer capitalism that has been uprooting worlds for the past century, with much earlier and deeper roots (see Moore 2017, 2018, Malm 2016), has learned to live with rights, while at the same time itself depending on their continuous infringement. Whether advocates like it or not, the rights of nature based on the history recounted here cannot but participate in this same world.

The history that I have presented so far is necessarily abbreviated and selective. However, it contains the main elements that have influenced rights of nature discourses so far. As the argument turns towards actual rights for nature, it will become easier to see how the elements presented here show up in practice. But this is not simply a matter of theory applying to practice. Rather, thinking and doing are always intertwined, one making the other possible. In turning to rights of nature laws and provisions, it will become clear how thinking occasioned the doing, but also how practice offers new ways of thinking, avenues that theory on its own could not have anticipated. Unsurprisingly, it is there that the actual contribution of Indigenous People is to be found, in the subtle resistance to rights and the equally subtle infiltration of truly novel ways of thinking about law, as well as the environing world.

The story of the rights of nature is being written, and will continue to be written for the foreseeable future. But the directions that it can evolve in are largely dependent on how theorists and practitioners reckon with the inheritance that seeps through the idea of rights for nature. I am myself committed to critiquing these rights such that they do not foreclose evolving in ways that cannot be currently anticipated. I am also committed to taking the rights of nature to task for unreflectively repeating histories of oppression. Lastly, I think it is prudent to always acknowledge one's fundamental ignorance and to let one's practice evolve in relationship with an enduringly mysterious environing world. Closely attending to practice means seeing one's ideas play out in the world. But it also means changing one's mind, as the uncertainty of the world generates new ideas.

Chapter III: From Theory to Practice[1]

Whereas the idea of giving nature rights started being systematically developed in the second part of the 20th century, its practice only really began in the 21st. So far, right provisions have appeared in different jurisdictions and at different legal levels, from municipal ordinances all the way to state constitutions themselves (arguably, the highest level of law). Currently, there are many different proposals being considered in yet more jurisdictions and at varying legal levels,[2] so I cannot hope to be exhaustive. Rather, I want to look at a representative sample of diverse rights for nature, such that we can begin to appreciate the diversity of practice and see how it makes new directions possible.

Municipal Ordinances

It may come as no surprise that the first deployment of rights of nature theory in practice occurred in the United States, a very impor-

1 Some parts of this chapter draw on a previously published article: Rights of Nature, Legal Personality, and Indigenous Philosophies, *Transnational Environmental Law*.

2 For a continuously updated list of cases, see https://www.therightsofnature.org/map-of-rights-of-nature. However, it is important to keep in mind that not all cases are the same, nor are they all unproblematically part of a "rights of nature movement". For a selective list of books on the rights of nature, see https://www.therightsofnature.org/related-books/. It is worth noting that these kinds of lists are not exhaustive, but largely focus on reinforcing the ecotheological strain of rights that is becoming orthodoxy.

tant node within their history. In 2006, Tamaqua Borough, Pennsylvania, adopted a municipal ordinance that granted rights to nature, understood as the area of the municipality. Sections 7.6, 7.7, and 12.2 of this ordinance bear obvious connections with the work of Christopher Stone, as they foreground the issue of standing as vitally important. But equally important is the background that led to this historic ordinance, which would repeat itself in dozens of other municipalities across the US.

The Tamaqua ordinance number 612 was specifically designed to oppose particular actions by corporations within the municipal area. The general area of the state of Pennsylvania where Tamaqua is located has for a long time been connected with resource exploitation, mostly mining. However, around the turn of this century, Tamaqua was facing a new threat in the form of the disposal of toxic sludge. Inasmuch as corporate actors would file all of the right paperwork, the disposal of the sludge could not be stopped. The argument that environmental regulation (in the US specifically, but not only) simply tells corporate actors how to best pollute had been a foundational one for the creation of the Community Legal Environmental Defense Fund (CELDF), a legal advocacy organization based in Pennsylvania that has advised on all similar municipal ordinances in the US so far, including the Tamaqua one.

CELDF has very consciously formed the rights of nature on the basis of the theory of Christopher Stone (resulting in a focus on legal standing), as well as the ecotheology of Berry and Cullinan (resulting in the idea of Nature as community). They have also been instrumental in presenting these rights as fundamentally countering the power of corporations, even though the instrument that they are trying to use – legal personality – is precisely the same instrument that corporations are using to wield their own legal power[3]

3 See Ciepley (2013) for more on the particularities of corporate personhood. CELDF are explicit in positioning the rights of nature as instruments against corporate personhood (also see Margil 2014 for an elaboration of their position). However, the basic instrument that corporations use – legal personality – is exactly the same in the case of rights for nature. This also means that, in some cases (see Chapters 4 and 6), the corporate person is the clos-

(see Chapter 5). It is important to recognize the outsized influence of CELDF on these particular municipal cases, as well as the way in which rights for nature are framed as evidently opposed to corporate power.

The Tamaqua ordinance originates in this ethos, so the relevant section (7.6) begins by specifically making it unlawful for "any corporation or its directors, officers, owners, or managers to interfere with the existence and flourishing of natural communities and ecosystems". The ordinance then goes on to repeatedly establish standing for both the municipal area (in itself), as well as for any resident of the borough to act as representative of the area's rights. This is summed up in declaring that "Borough residents, natural communities, and ecosystems shall be considered to be 'persons' for purposes of the enforcement of the civil rights of those residents, natural communities, and ecosystems".

The link between legal personality, rights, and standing is fully visible here. Lastly, the ordinance also grants all residents of the Borough "a fundamental and inalienable right to a healthy environment". This kind of third generation human right very often accompanies rights of nature, the assumption being that they are mutually reinforcing: where nature has rights, people's right to a good environment (however that may be defined) stands a better chance of being respected. However, rights of nature and *to* nature can also be in tension, especially inasmuch as it remains unclear just what rights nature may have in any given case, and which human groups have the power to determine the content of nature's rights as well as the content of human rights to nature. This first practical appearance of rights for nature raises more questions than it answers, but through the advocacy of CELDF it became a very important blueprint for later ordinances, and indeed for the first constitutional rights of nature in history (see next section).

Among the many questions raised by this formulation of rights for nature there are two that I find particularly important. First,

---

est analogy to the personhood of nature. Whether this works with or against corporate power is an open question and certainly not decided by the instrument of rights (or legal personality) as such.

the ordinance clearly wants to establish a kind of nature's right to restoration, which in principle is understandable and laudable. However, this kind of right starts to show the limitations of the underlying concept of nature as an eco*system*, that is to say a *community* that is naturally in *balance*. This idea of Nature, which we started to explore in the previous chapter, forces restoration to be done according to a baseline, that is to say to a standard that is fixed by human observation of an environment at a particular time. In the case of the ordinance under discussion here, the municipal law states that restoration should be done for the benefit of the "natural community" by reverting said community to a pre-disturbance state.

Two fundamental issues complicate the idea of baseline restoration considerably. In the context of climate change, reverting to a baseline may prove impossible. This, in a more general way, has always been the case, because natural processes are by definition dynamic; they therefore change all the time. With the added dynamism injected into natural processes by a hefty amount of extra atmospheric CO_2, baseline restoration becomes not much more than a wish. In addition, there is no clear way of choosing a baseline. Given that this concept is fundamentally historical (that is, it requires going back in time to choose a preferred state), there are no pre-determined criteria for choosing one particular moment in history over another. Imagine, then, that an old coal pit, abandoned many decades ago, has become an oasis for local birds. Would this particular place, if affected by the actions of a corporate actor presently, have to be reverted to being an abandoned coal pit, or to some other pre-mining state? If the latter, then which state? Before or after the colonial enclosure of land that created the current Borough 'locals'?

The second question raised by this ordinance is that of the relationship between local people and local nature. There seems to be an operating assumption of locals being friendly to the natural environment, which is the only way of accounting for the granting of standing to residents. But what if a shareholder of a corporation invested in toxic sludge becomes a resident of the Borough? According to the law, there would be nothing to stop her from acting on behalf of nature, and arguing, for example, that a certain amount of sewage sludge, on account of its chemical composition, is to the benefit of the natural community. The corporation itself, as a legal person, could become resident of the Borough, in which case the situation would become even more complicated.

I point these issues out to give an idea of the complexities that are raised when the conceptual apparatus that we saw in the last chapter is simply applied to a case, as if said case had a duty to conform to the theory. As things stand, corporate actors have not had to become local residents in order to dismantle these kinds of laws from within. The level of the law – municipal – has made these but unenforceable. Macpherson (2021a) shows how these laws have been consistently opposed, and sometimes struck down, in court. Courts have taken the view that these kinds of municipal ordinances are unconstitutional, on various grounds. Some scholars (Fitz-Henry 2018) argue that the whole point of these municipal ordinances is to contest the terrain of legal personality, by showing that if corporations can be legal persons, so can nature. That may be so, but that doesn't solve the moral/legal conundrums we have already started to explore, nor the problem with the vague formulations, at municipal level, that seem to not be able to pass into higher levels of the law. Neither does it offer a convincing case for how the rights of nature could be environmentally beneficial.

The recipe first developed in Tamaqua was applied by CELDF in dozens of different communities across the US.[4] The basic conceptual apparatus remains largely unchanged throughout them. Chapters 5 and 6 will interrogate this apparatus much closer, especially paying attention to the concept of nature and the kinds of rights that it is assigned. This way of thinking rights of nature has become very influential, particularly in cases that focus on *rights*, and in particular on what could be called existence rights (Macpherson 2021), namely the claim that an ecosystem has to continue in a particular form. The most ambitious, and so far influential, of these cases

4 See https://celdf.org/community-rights/ for updated cases of community ordinances in the United States.

has been the 2008 constitution of Ecuador, the first in the world to recognize such rights.

Constitutional Rights for Nature in Ecuador

In the context of a leftist and populist government, spearheaded by Rafael Correa, Ecuador rewrote its constitution (for the 20th time in its history) and adopted a new founding text in 2008. The writing of the new constitution was accomplished through the establishment of a Constitutional Assembly, tasked with drafting the document through a series of remarkably participative consultations. The seat of the Assembly was in the city of Montecristi, and for most of its work it was led by Ecuadorian academic, economist, and politician Alberto Acosta.

I detailed the precise working of the rights of nature through the Constitutional Assembly in Tănăsescu (2013, 2016). There is no need to recall all of the details here. Instead, I want to pick out, as before, the constitutive elements of the constitutional rights of nature in this case. But in order to do so, it is important to establish the particular intellectual genealogy that led to including them in the constitution in the first place. After all, this is the first time it has ever happened, and it is therefore important to try to understand why they appeared in this form at this particular historical conjunction.

One of the keys to understanding this historical moment is to grasp the role of the Assembly president, Alberto Acosta.[5] Throughout his career, Acosta went from more or less mainstream economist to a pioneer of environmental thinking in Ecuador. Since the Assembly was called into existence, Acosta has published influential pieces on the necessity to grant rights to nature in order to achieve true environmental protection. In this, he collaborated closely with Eduardo Gudynas, a Uruguayan prolific proponent of

5 Acosta started his term as Assembly president, but did not finish it. He resigned in protest as what he saw as political interference, but this was after the passage of the rights of nature was assured.

'biocentrism', and Esperanza Martinez, the leader of one of the most influential Ecuadorian environmental NGOs, Acción Ecologica. Together, they have also been instrumental in proposing and supporting campaigns for ending oil exploitation in the Amazon region of Ecuador (for example Acosta et al 2009), as well as instituting a new regime of development around the concept of Sumak Kawsay, or "good living".[6] His role as a power broker in the Constitutional Assembly is crucial for understanding the genesis of rights for nature in Ecuador.

Through the figure of Acosta, several histories we have seen in the previous chapter coalesced and mixed with new, specifically Ecuadorian, elements in order to create a version of rights of nature that has become, arguably, the most influential to date. Though Acosta himself (Acosta 2010) has claimed that he was not familiar with previous work on rights of nature, other sources (Kauffman and Martin 2017a,b) claim that, through personal relationships he was acquainted with the work of Stone as well as that of Jörg Leimbacher. Leimbacher was a Swiss jurist that wrote a 1988 book on rights for nature, *Die Rechte der Natur*, a decidedly early contribution to the field.

However that kind of personal influence may have developed, two things are certain. First, in strictly conceptual terms Acosta's idea of rights of nature closely grafts unto some of the influential predecessors discussed in the previous chapter, particularly those of the ecotheological strand. Second, whatever he might have been familiar with before the Assembly, it is certain that through presiding over the Assembly and afterwards, he came into close contact with several influential activists for rights that were steeped in the same ecotheological tradition. The most important of these was CELDF.

This organization, together with Fundación Pachamama (whose co-founder, Bill Twist, introduced Acosta to CELDF), played a very

6 Also codified in the 2008 Constitution, which recognizes the Quechua principle of Sumak Kawsay, translated in Spanish as buen vivir (living well). This principle is supposed to give a framework to the whole constitution and is based on a model of well-being that is not driven by economic indicators only. See Kowii (2009), Acosta (2013).

important role in drafting the constitutional articles dealing with rights of nature. Farith Simon (2019) went as far as claiming that CELDF themselves drafted the constitutional provisions. Certainly, there are obvious congruences between the organization's work with municipal ordinances and the articles enshrining rights for nature in Ecuador's constitution. The similarities between the Ecuadorian provisions and the US municipal ordinances do not stem from an underlying unity that these kinds of rights have, but rather from the direct influence of the same people and the same intellectual sources in all of these cases. Ecuador, no less than the municipal ordinances, is a direct inheritor of the strand of rights that heavily draws on the ecotheology of Nature as a Subject to be recognized by law. Here are the Ecuadorian constitutional provisions:

> **Art. 71.** Nature, or Pachamama, where life is reproduced and occurs, has the right to integral respect for its existence and for the maintenance and regeneration of its life cycles, structure, functions and evolutionary processes.
> All persons, communities, peoples and nations can demand public authorities enforce the rights of nature. To enforce and interpret these rights, the principles set forth in the Constitution shall be observed, as appropriate.
> The State shall give incentives to natural persons and legal entities and to communities to protect nature and to promote respect for all the elements comprising an ecosystem.
>
> **Art. 72.** Nature has the right to be restored. This restoration shall be apart from the obligation of the State and natural persons or legal entities to compensate individuals and communities that depend on affected natural systems.
> In those cases of severe or permanent environmental impact, including those caused by the exploitation of nonrenewable natural resources, the State shall establish the most effective mechanisms to achieve the restoration and shall adopt adequate measures to eliminate or mitigate harmful environmental consequences.
>
> **Art. 73.** The State shall apply preventive and restrictive measures on activities that might lead to the extinction of species, the de-

struction of ecosystems and the permanent alteration of natural cycles.
The introduction of organisms and organic and inorganic material that might definitively alter the nation's genetic assets is forbidden.

Art. 74. Persons, communities, peoples, and nationalities shall have the right to benefit from the environment and the natural wealth enabling them to enjoy the good living.
Environmental services shall not be subject to appropriation; their production, delivery, use and development shall be regulated by the State.

Exactly as in the case of Tamaqua Borough, much care is taken to codify rights in terms of Berry's fundamental right to existence, as well as to specifically address the issue of standing that was so central to Cristopher Stone. Whereas in the case of Tamaqua being specific about standing was made necessary by the level of the law, in a constitutional formulation this is not the case. Given that the constitution is the highest law of the land, standing is automatically given to whatever legal personality the document inaugurates. So, focusing explicitly on standing is strictly speaking redundant, but it shows very well the particular intellectual genealogy that plays out in practice. As in the case of the municipal ordinances, standing is codified in the largest possible sense. Whereas in the municipal case standing applied to any resident, here it applies to any person whatsoever, even regardless of nationality.[7] Besides this issue, the duality of rights *for* (Art. 72) and *to* (Art. 74) nature is also present. Finally, the issue of restoration appears as a fundamental right, though none of the problems explored in the earlier section are resolved.

The dominance of rights as *the* tools of emancipation is undeniable in the Ecuadorian constitution writ large. The radically participatory process that the Constitutional Assembly had set up for

7 In Tănăsescu (2016) I developed at much greater length the discussion of the universality of standing, as well as documenting in detail the political process within the Constitutional Assembly. The reader interested in the Ecuadorian case specifically should also consult that work.

drafting the new document was somehow corralled into rights language at every turn. There are, importantly, many indigenous rights to their own territories and traditions. The panoply of rights (including, among others, to "healthy, sufficient and nutritious food; preferably produced locally and in accord with various identities and cultural traditions"; art.12, 13) cannot but reinforce the power of the state, which is ultimately tasked with upholding them. The Constitution seems to think that there can be no conflict between different kinds of rights, and simply states that if such conflicts arise, they will be dealt with appropriately (art. 85/2). Exactly how this may be done remains an open question, but that the state will be the primary mover in resolving such conflicts is very likely, to say the least.

The power of the state, and the role that rights play in safeguarding it, is nowhere clearer than in the relegation of mineral rights to the state itself (as well as the right to control energy production, water and biodiversity; art. 313). This apparently post-extractivist document allocates the rights that can make a difference to the project of modern development and its inherent depredations to a state deeply committed to resource extraction. Indigenous Nationalities, which otherwise receive rights to their territories, have no veto power over extractive activities in their own lands, and therefore have no effective property rights at all (arguably the paradigmatic rights of the liberal order). On a smaller scale, the tension between different kinds of rights and their role in unequal power distributions is also visible in the rights of nature provisions themselves, where these rights are presented as inherently compatible with people's rights to nature. There are many cases one can imagine where there is no such compatibility, but the point is that treating these rights as inherently friendly towards each other allows state power to become the ultimate arbiter, and therefore to use the rights of nature selectively.

As I and others have already argued (for example Rawson and Mansfield 2018), the rights of nature in Ecuador were forged through a particular power constellation that reunited elite actors from the governmental and NGO worlds. Though many of these actors have consistently claimed that the rights of nature are part of a global movement, the case of Ecuador seems rather an elite-driven project that, for contingent historical reasons, was successful. That being said, the Ecuadorian case and its particular power constellation also contributed to developing the rights of nature in ways that were previously absent. In particular, the participation of the organized Indigenous movements (especially CONAIE, the largest Indigenous organization in the country) within the Assembly, as key partners in Correa's government, left a deep mark on the constitution, as well as on the now-orthodox interpretation of rights of nature as of indigenous inspiration.

Despite the well-documented Indigenous involvement in the Constitutional Assembly, the power brokers behind the rights of nature provisions remained white settler elites. It is this group that interpreted Pachamama as a kind of Gaia, as the community that Berry and Stutzin assumed the natural world to be. For particular Indigenous People, it is often territories, *with particular names*, that feature as abodes, friends, relatives, kin in the struggle and joy that is life. As I have argued elsewhere (Tănăsescu 2020, but also see Macpherson 2021), indigenous philosophies are primarily *relational*, that is to say that they do not recognize intrinsic values as such, but rather focus on the development of situated relationships with natural beings that are always in flux. This is also why indigenous philosophies are not, by and large, ecocentric: they do not posit a nature that is prior to its relationships, nor do they see the inherent value of nature as opposed to the use humans may make of it.

Much of what gives purchase to the idea of the rights of nature being indigenous in some sense is the notion of harmony, in a double sense: on the one hand, harmony as obtaining between Indigenous People and nature (a colonial conceptual inheritance), and harmony as inhering in nature itself (an inheritance from the early days of ecology and its uptake into ecotheology). On both of these counts, the idea of harmony is misleading. First, it is not the case that Indigenous People are inherently in harmony with nature. This of course does not mean that they are inherently destructive of nature, but it does mean that they have diverse histories which do not, definitionally, exclude a variety of relationships with the natural world. To substantiate this point, it suffices to recall that, according to the overwhelming evidence that we currently have, the great megafauna extinction at the end of the last ice age occurred when all human groups, from the vantage of contemporary modernity, were 'indigenous'.

Second, the idea of nature as inherently balanced is not obviously of indigenous origins. It is true that many Indigenous People refer to their environment as in balance, but this claim is open to diverse interpretations. One can interpret it as meaning that these groups share an Odum-like idea of ecosystems as striving towards balance. But it can also be interpreted in culturally specific ways as indicating a particular kind of relationship with the land, where the idea of balance is a heuristic for making sense of human and natural actions alike. The idea of balance interpreted thus refers to the reciprocity of relationships between natural and human actors. What is in balance is *the economy of exchange*, not the *form* of the environment itself (which is how western philosophy and science interprets balance). The form of the environment is forever changing, and this is reflected in much indigenous mythology quite explicitly: the world is that which has transformed many times over and continues to transform. The idea of balance is a way of indicating how humans are to participate in the perpetual transformations *that they do not lead*, in such a way as to secure their continued subsistence.

Though in much rights of nature literature harmony and balance are treated as synonymous, there is yet another way of thinking about harmony that may indeed resonate with some indigenous conceptions. Harmony, in its musical sense, is the idea that sounds can fit together in ways that are pleasant to listen to, that seem to cohere as if they belonged in that particular formation. Similarly, Andean indigenous philosophies, for example, do employ the idea that humans can be in harmony with their surroundings, in the sense of fitting well, or belonging to each other. But this sense of harmony is as dynamic as the natural world itself, and periods of disharmony are as natural as periods of coherence, inasmuch as human groups must continuously adapt to an often temperamental and forever dynamic nature. In the Western appropriation of harmony, the dynamism of the indigenous world is often lost and replaced by the ecological idea of balance, or by the colonial inheritance of an inherently benign population.

The idea of balance does not sit well within the baseline-driven restoration that rights of nature in this form propose because it is not about the outlines (for example, species composition) of a territory and its precise makeup, but rather about the endurance and perpetuation of particular kinds of exchanges and relationships across kinds of beings.[8] An indigenous-inspired restoration would therefore aim at restoring the kinds of generative and reciprocal relationships that are the basis of many indigenous cultures, rather than the form of a particular environment (this is exactly what Tāmati Kruger, Tūhoe leader, advocates for in the case of Te Urewera; see next Chapter). It remains an open question what the precise legal formulation of this ethos may be, but it is far from obvious that giving rights to nature is it. In fact, the ecotheological version of nature's rights doesn't quite seem up to the task of facilitating Indigenous legal autonomy. Instead, we may be better served by thinking about how to allow those already existing legal traditions to gain more power and to introduce ideas that may have nothing to do with personhood, or rights, at all.

As it may have become clear, despite the claims of many rights advocates, these laws cannot be primarily about 'nature', but rather about who has power over what and in what form (see Chapters 6 and 7). Now, I want to continue painting the picture of the most important cases of rights of nature so far, such that we may move away from the dominance of ecotheology and towards new possibilities.

The Law of Mother Earth, Bolivia

Not long after the Ecuadorian case, Bolivia followed suit by adopting a national law granting rights to nature, the 2010 Law of Mother Earth (Ley de Derechos de la Madre Tierra). As in the case of Ecuador before, the Bolivian law draws heavily on the dominant history already explored, as well as bringing new elements to the table. In particular, the Bolivian law takes the splicing of rights for nature

8 I discuss this at large in *Ecocene Politics* (2022). This idea is also given purchase by De Castro's concept of multinaturalism (2019, 2014b).

and indigeneity a step further and is therefore a very good one to analyze in order to attempt to parse out the very complicated relationship between Indigenous groups and state law in general, as well as rights in particular.

The Bolivian law, adopted in December 2010, starts with a long preamble that establishes its general context and the definition of Mother Earth as an interconnected whole comprising all living systems and beings, understood as inextricably linked and complementary. In terms of the analytical tools already developed, this is clearly a capital letter concept of Nature, at the highest level of abstraction. It also clearly reflects the idea that Nature is in balance, here expressed through the concept of complementarity. I want to stress again that this is *not* an ecological concept of nature. In ecology, extinctions and what are called 'disturbances' are commonplace (see Chapter 2). In fact, the vast majority of everything that has ever lived has already gone extinct. This doesn't let people off the hook for their share of responsibility, but it does suggest that Nature is not the only concept available. Instead, when we see this concept we have to ask what it is *doing*, instead of assuming that it is an accurate description of a 'deeper' way of understanding the world.

The Bolivian law, which goes on to grant the same right to restoration that we saw earlier, is distinctive in two ways. First, it refers to Mother Earth, clearly introducing the issue of gender within rights of nature in a way that is merely implied elsewhere. Second, it connects indigenous thinking to the figure of Mother Earth. These two issues need to be tackled together.

Unlike rights of nature in Ecuador that did not enjoy the support of then president, Rafael Correa, the rights in Bolivia were widely and loudly promoted by then president, Evo Morales, himself a member of the Aymara Indigenous community. His own identity as Indigenous leader, besides national president, already did much to cement a close identification of Bolivian rights of nature with indigenous views. In speeches, Morales routinely referred to Mother Earth and Pachamama, the Andean deity, as synonymous and drew explicit parallels between the two, as if the idea of Mother Earth was the unproblematic translation of Pachamama.

When taking a closer look at the law itself, the first thing to notice is that the term Pachamama does not appear at all. This is very different from Ecuador, where Pachamama appears as a clear synonym of Nature in the constitutional text. But in the Bolivian case, the law only speaks about Mother Earth, and simply mentions, once, that this figure is sacred in the 'cosmovision' of Indigenous People. If looked at in its context, the law can be – and has been – interpreted to have given rights to Pachamama, just like in Ecuador. But this is not supported by the legal text itself.

Why does this matter? Because paying attention to *how* indigenous thought is used in rights of nature laws is important in understanding *why* it is used, and how that may affect Indigenous communities themselves, as well as various environments. It matters, in other words, because close attention can demystify claims that may end up working against Indigenous self-determination, as well as against various environments. In the case of Bolivia in particular, the figure of Pachamama is presented as a mother figure, and therefore first and foremost a stereotypically nurturing female (see Tola 2018 for a critique). The association between Pachamama and motherhood was further supported by the proposal submitted by Morales to the UN to pass a Universal Declaration of the Rights of Mother Earth, modeled on the Universal Declaration of Human Rights. This proposal had behind it many of the same power brokers we saw in Ecuador.

It may be that the identification of an Andean deity with a gendered concept of Nature is supported by indigenous philosophies themselves. Or it may be that this particular association is strategic for all involved, whether for Indigenous organizations themselves or for NGOs or other actors in the transnational network of rights of nature. In order to be able to ascertain this, I need to take a closer look at the concept of Pachamama, as well as how the concept of Nature attempts to translate a vision that sits very uncomfortably within the dominant laws of the state.

Pachamama as Female Nature

There are two ways of accounting for differences between culturally specific ways of understanding the world. The first sees these differences as ones of degree, that is to say that there are different *views* on the *same* world. This is the dominant, Western way of understanding cultural differences, and one that informed colonialism deeply, from the practice of religious conversion to the imposition of legal orders that had nothing to do with indigenous concepts. The other way of understanding difference is as difference of *kind*, that is to say that there are fundamentally different *worlds* that are being perceived, and not just views on the same world. Incidentally, this is the view that most Indigenous communities have themselves supported through centuries of colonialism, insisting that Western men failed to *see* certain features of a world that is fundamentally different from the Western one.

What does it mean for there to be multiple worlds? First of all, it means that the beings that populate worlds are fundamentally different. In the Western understanding of world, this is only populated by beings whose sentience is decided upon through scientific methods of controlled observation. In the Andean world, there are many kinds of beings that, through the scientific method, people could not even begin to detect. Marisol de la Cadena speaks, for example, of Earth Beings, entities that to westerners look like 'landscape features' but that, to Indigenous locals, are active and sentient in their own right.

The point is not to decide which view is right, but to recognize that we are really speaking about qualitatively different worlds. In the same breath, it becomes important to recognize that the cultural underpinning of colonialism is precisely the project of replacing one world for another, so that the claim of a single world accepting of different views can finally prevail (multiculturalism replacing multinaturalism). As Moana Jackson (1992) argues, "the history of colonization […] is a story of the imposition of philosophical construct as much as it is a tale of economic and military oppression" (2).

One of the theorists that has done most to make the case for the existence of qualitatively different worlds is Brazilian anthropologist Eduardo Viveiros de Castro. However, much of the anthropological corpus can be read precisely as a record of misunderstanding the nature of the ontological difference between different groups of people. De Castro speaks about *equivocation*, which de la Cadena (2015) understands as "not [...] a simple failure to understand. Rather it is 'a failure to understand that understandings are *necessarily* not the same, and that they *are not related* to imaginary ways of 'seeing the world' *but to the real worlds that are being seen*'." This is exactly what I referred to above as a difference of kind. She continues: "as a mode of communication, equivocations emerge when different perspectival positions – views *from* different worlds, rather than perspectives about the same world – use the same word to refer to things that are not the same" (110).

The supposed equivalence between Nature and Pachamama can be seen exactly as this kind of equivocation, a supposed equivalence of perspective about a fundamentally similar world, when in fact they convey radically different worlds. Nature, as I have explored throughout, is quintessentially modernist and, surely despite the best intentions of many advocates, cannot help but perpetuate colonial relations aimed at cultural erasure. It is ironic that many rights of nature advocates contrast Nature with the idea of resource, as if the first recognizes something special while the latter does nothing but flatten the world. In fact, these two notions share exactly the same structure, as they work at the same level of abstraction. There is no such thing as Nature in itself, just as there is no such thing as 'a resource'. There are many different things that are flattened and smashed together by the dominant idea of 'resource' (there are always infinite variations in woods, coal, oil, gas, kinds of foods, whatever may be the case). The idea of Nature is a radical oversimplification of worlds (just like resource is a radical oversimplification of affordances), which are always so complex and fundamentally mysterious as to resist – for careful cultures – being simplified within one single concept.[9] And there are many different worlds that are flattened and smashed together by the idea of Nature.

This is because Nature is a concept that can only arise out of cultures seeking universality, and hence justifications for their right to rule over everything. This kind of colonial thrust cannot be undone by using the same conceptual apparatus that is fundamental in propelling it! Nature is a globalist, universalist, totalizing concept that has nothing to do with any particular place. It has no features as such, which is why it can only be associated with vague and stereotypical features that unfailingly reproduce state power. It is in this sense that the supposed femininity of Nature arises. There is nothing obviously 'female' about 'Nature', and many indigenous cultures – Andean ones included – have a much more nuanced view of gendered pairings, as some places are perceived as female while other as male,[10] while others still as both. But Nature as One unifying concept has to choose, and it chooses for whatever helps state power most.

The figure of Mother Earth feeds on, and into, the stereotypical portrayal of femininity as nurturing and caring. Whether or not this conforms to the character of the natural world is a moot point, but the issue of caring deserves some discussion. The natural world is and has always been (to the vast majority of cultures everywhere) a capricious one. Even if it was conceived as feminine in some sense, and in some cases, it was a feminine that could kill as well as bring forth life. The capriciousness of nature is seen in the destructive events that, from the point of view of creatures, seem to come from nowhere and interrupt life as it had previously existed. This is why Isabelle Stengers (2015) calls the current era of concern with natural processes an "intrusion", that is to say something that invades with no regard for anyone's will. But she does not speak about the intrusion of Nature, but rather of Gaia, a mythical figure that, precisely because of its divinity, could do whatever it pleases with human life.

---

9 If we want a theological argument for this, we can look at Wendell Berry's work.

10 In Māori mythology, for example, Ranginui is the sky *father*. See Salmond (2017).

Nature in this sense is not caring, but rather powerful enough to be indifferent. Human matters are none of its concern, which is precisely why it has to be appeased, because of its tremendous power and the arbitrariness with which it wields it. Natural processes intrude, and this is a truth that us moderns have afforded, temporarily, to forget. The whole project of modernity can be seen as an absurd plan to escape natural constraints, which for a while seemed to work. It at least worked to such an extent that it allowed moderns to disregard the capriciousness of the surrounding world, an awesome force that they shut out through different kinds of insurance: abundance, control, inventiveness of technique. But Gaia, sooner or later, intrudes, and the current era is precisely that time when moderns can no longer afford their illusions.

This is why some may think of nature as revengeful, which at least has the benefit of recognising natural violence and avoiding motherly abstractions. Revenge itself may not be, in the final analysis, a better way of conceiving the enveloping world, largely because indifference manages to account for more of its facets. It is hard to believe that whole species would be wiped out because of nature taking revenge, particularly because the image of the revengeful goddess seems to be accompanied by an idealisation of animal life: the goddess takes revenge on humans for having fallen from animal grace. Perhaps it is because of the successful erasure of cultural memory that moderns have started entertaining the idea that nature can be imagined as Mother Earth.

Is nature nurturing? In a sense, yes; it is the precondition of life. But this is banal, tautological: Nature (the interrelated processes of life) is the basis of life. Inasmuch as there is no life outside of 'nature', this version of nurturing is not very helpful. Instead, it may seem nurturing in that it offers things that many life forms find useful. But its capriciousness interrupts the gift, which can be withheld at any moment: going from abundance to scarcity, favourable to unfavourable conditions, life to death. This is but the condition of life as such.

'Mother Earth' does not describe a reality, whether ecological or cultural, but repeats unconscious modern tropes in a way that is ultimately unthreatening to wider power relations that are still predicated on overcoming natural limitations to life.

As Tola (2018) shows carefully, the idea that nature is female works well with the idea of resource exploitation, because resources are exactly what the femininity of nature produces. And these resources then stand to be appropriated by the state as 'gifts of nature'. This is very ironic, especially if we consider that all of the legal documents surveyed in this chapter frame the rights of nature as intrinsically opposed to resource exploitation. The intentions of many activists involved in these legal texts are of course anti-extractivist! But the conceptual apparatus that they rely on, with roots explored in the previous chapter, hampers their efforts. This is not merely a theoretical argument. It remains the case, empirically, that both Ecuador and Bolivia have expanded their extractive industries considerably since passing rights of nature laws (see Chapter 6).The law itself, especially formulated in the way that we have seen so far, is mostly impotent in the face of state power. Rights for nature are first and foremost politics, and the concepts they use are key in understanding how they inscribe themselves in already existing power struggles.

The idea of Pachamama is a kind of touristification of Andean thinking. It is important to recognize that there are many Andean worlds and that the choice of indigenous terms already favors certain dominant communities (like the Aymara and the Quechua) over others. But even in its generalized form (that is, the form specifically crafted to resemble the universality of Nature), Pachamama is not a deity in the Christian sense, nor is it equivalent (another *view*) to Nature. Instead, Pachamama reunites many different terms (in different Andean languages) that more or less refer to the spirit that animates life, the suchness of being that is indescribable yet crucial for there to be anything at all. Many communities that live in intricately close relationships with their places recognize the basic fact that humans are not responsible for life processes, but rather are beneficiaries of these. Life processes themselves transcend human powers and make humans subordinate and, in a very real sense, dependent on their gifts. But the expression of the spirit of life, as it were, is apprehended through local things and situations.

Indigenous conceptions tend to reflect the observable phenomenon that life communities differ greatly according to location. To suppose that they all express the same 'life spirit' is precisely to assimilate these views to a universalist Nature that a-modern societies do not tend to recognize. The life spirit that animates the beings of Māori, Sami, or Aymara only looks the same from the perspective of a modernist mind that already presupposes the existence of underlying sameness (*one* world).

De la Cadena (2015), in discussing Aymara thought in modern Peru, does not speak of Pachamama, but rather of *pukara,* which she characterizes (taking care to note that it is still an epistemic translation, and not her personal practice) as "a source of life, a condition for the relational entanglement that is the world of ayllu" (108). The concept of *ayllu,* a crucial one for the communities she worked with, designates the ensemble of beings that makes a place and through which pukara can be expressed. This concept, though crucial for Andean thought, is completely absent from rights of nature, because it is fundamentally local. You cannot have a universal declaration of the rights of ayllu, though it is through the recognition of ayllu authority that radically different legal and political orders may become possible.

De la Cadena is very careful to show the crucial misalignment between the expansion of the modern state (in this case, in Peru) and ayllu. Even when leftist politicians, like in the case of the agrarian reforms in the mid-20th century in Peru, adopt the concept, they mean something else, precisely because of their ontological universalism. Nobody is more acutely aware of these misalignments, and of their immediate consequences, than Indigenous People themselves. The question then arises: why have Indigenous organizations in both Ecuador and Bolivia supported the idea of granting rights to nature?

The most important thing to keep in mind in answering this question is that Indigenous communities are not timeless, changeless groupings. This is how they have been imagined throughout colonial history. We have seen that Sharma (2020) argues that the idea that Indigenous People naturally belong to certain places was instrumental in the development of the nation state and in extending the state's power and control over all national territories (Indigenous reservations included). Not incidentally, rights discourses were important in the spread of national power from the beginning. Already in the 19th century, Western advocates for indigenous rights argued that Indigenous People needed to be protected by the state by being given rights to their particular places, from which they could not deviate. This was a mechanism of enclosure much more than a mechanism of granting meaningful recognition of the special, place-based relationships that often obtained between Indigenous People and places.

Historically, Indigenous People have moved about, like all human populations have, for millennia. The progress of colonialism and modernity has fixed the survivors in place, while making it almost impossible to realize the wealth of a-modern experiences and conceptions that have completely disappeared. In other words, Indigenous People today have been in the direct firing line of state power for centuries and are therefore very well versed in dealing with this power that always threatens their survival and that has routinely relegated them to what the state perceived as marginal lands. From an indigenous perspective, this is the background on which nature's rights appear. It is not as if in 2006 with the passage of the Tamaqua Borough ordinance, something was born in the world that finally gave Indigenous People tools to fight the state. Instead, the rights of nature are one of the latest expansions of state power into indigenous worlds, one that is much better in many ways than other alternatives, but one that does nothing to fundamentally challenge the power of the state (the one, in the final analysis, responsible for upholding rights).

With the exception of isolated tribes in the Amazon rainforest that have *chosen* not to engage with the modern world, all other Indigenous communities have been tasked for centuries with mastering a fine dance with the state, a dance that their survival depends on. From a modernist perspective, rights of nature seen as indigenous tradition made state law have accomplished a historic task. From an indigenous perspective, these rights are the next episode in a long series of nation-state capture of indigenous practice and thought. The Indigenous leaders involved in this capture understand that their apparent acquiescence to the terms of the state merely prepares the ground for the next round of conflict, for new demands that are made possible by the laying of another layer to the fundamentally conflictual history of Indigenous-state relations.

From Nature to Places, from Rights to Representation

If the point of the rights of nature is to move beyond modernist law, then the concept of nature might be an even bigger problem than the concept of rights. But the rights of nature are not limited to the history and practice so far explored. This modernist, universalist strand of rights has been quite successful so far, but it is not alone. There are other cases that have started to show radically new possibilities, not least because they are anchored in specific places as opposed to relying on the concept of Nature. Though on the face of it municipal ordinances in the US are of this kind, this is not so. Tamaqua Borough is simply a stand-in for Nature, but because the law is a municipal ordinance, it had to be 'reduced' to the area of the municipality. The municipality has no features at all, it is modernist flat space defined in an administrative way ('the municipality') and in relation to another administrative unit ('the resident').

Instead, there are a growing number of cases of rights for nature given to beings with their own names and specific features. Key among these have been a series of rivers, which is not surprising given how sentient they have appeared to many different cultures throughout history. Whanganui river in Aotearoa New Zealand is perhaps the most famous of these, but legal personality arrangements have also been proposed in relation to Ganga and Yamuna rivers in India, Atrato river in Colombia, and all rivers in Bangladesh. Besides these, Lake Eerie in the United State has had a short stint as a legal person,[11] while discussions are ongoing for legal personality arrangements for a Lagoon in Spain, a wetland in

11 The rights of Lake Eerie were quickly struck down by higher courts (Macpherson 2021a).

Florida, and aquatic ecosystems as such in Europe, to name but the latest ones.

As I have shown in the case of Tamaqua, it is not enough to specify the name of a place in order to propose legal alternatives that make a decisive break with modernist conceptions. In other words, it is very much possible to have ecotheological rights for nature applied to particular places. What makes the situation analytically difficult is that a staggering number of conceptual combinations are theoretically and practically possible. As I will show later, when discussing the case of the Indian and Colombian rivers, many elements encountered so far are applied to those places as well. There we can witness a combination of apparently contradictory movements: totality thinking applied to particular places. The key to understanding this apparent contradiction is to see legal personality arrangements and rights of nature as always political moves that apportion power in different ways.

Besides the way in which nature is understood and legally codified, equally important is who has the power to represent it, and why. This issue is at the heart of all rights of nature; it is where the theoretical rubber hits the very practical road. In Tănăsescu (2016), I developed this aspect of rights of nature as being about who has the right to represent a nature with rights, and I still think it is a fruitful way of thinking about these rights as mechanisms of representation for newly created legal and political entities. The issue of representation is crucial precisely because of the conceptual tangles that I have so far tried to make clear: Who has the right to speak on behalf of Ecuador's nature has everything to do with the kinds of things that can be accomplished.

Similarly, granting rights to a specific entity (as opposed to nature as such) may continue reproducing power inequities inasmuch as the law remains vague as to who has the power to represent the newly created legal entity. In some cases, the representatives are specified, but the reasons for choosing them, as opposed to others, are opaque. If the rights of nature are always about who has the power to speak, then we must always ask for the reasons a certain group may be preferred over another (also see Tănăsescu 2021). It also matters how the law allows for a change in representatives if certain goals are not achieved. Finally, the issue of representation is the most promising one for accommodating legal pluralism, namely the meeting, on equal terms, of indigenous and western legal conceptions.

The ecotheological strand of rights unites the totality of Nature with that of Rights. Practice has started to show that these can be separated by applying rights to distinct places. But the most interesting and promising alternative is a complete divorce from totalities as such by focusing on legal status and representative arrangements instead of rights and general nature. There are several cases that exemplify most successfully the way in which a territory is related to its inhabitants, and the potential of thinking locally together with groups that are privileged in representing new legal entities. This is the case of Te Urewera, the home of Tūhoe in Aotearoa New Zealand and the first case of rights for nature in that country. Let us examine it in detail.

Chapter IV: Diversity of Practice[1]

Both in theory and in practice, a dominant, orthodox view of the rights of nature has developed. I have shown how it has been built through the advocacy of a transnational policy network, drawing on an ecotheological tradition steeped in liberal rights advocacy. The coherence of a potential movement for rights of nature is, however, questioned by the appearance of cases that diverge significantly from the conceptual contours explored thus far. Several cases in Aotearoa[2] New Zealand are markedly different from the ones already seen, also in the sense that they do not share the same intellectual history. It is worth looking at these carefully. I want to start with what I find to be the most extraordinary case of rights of nature so far, namely the passage of Te Urewera[3] from a national park to the status of self-owning legal entity.

The 2014 law that accomplished this passage deserves detailed examination, for several reasons. Despite the fact that Te Urewera precedes the Whanganui river Act (2017), the latter has become

1 This chapter draws in part on a previously published article: Rights of Nature, Legal Personality, and Indigenous Philosophies, *Transnational Environmental Law*.

2 Māori name for New Zealand.

3 This is the name of a part of the North Island that is home to Tūhoe, a Māori group that has had the most conflictual history with the settler state. Until well into the 20th century, lands were confiscated and Tūhoe leaders and political activists persecuted. Today, this part of New Zealand is still seen as a mysterious place. Te Urewera is a vast area of mountainous forested landscapes, often shrouded in mist. Tūhoe call themselves the children of the mist.

much more famous internationally. This is perhaps because rivers exert a certain pull on the imagination, whereas Te Urewera is only significant to outsiders if one digs a bit deeper, as that name on its own doesn't say much to people not already familiar with it. Its relative obscurity notwithstanding, this case is radical in the way in which it departs from rights orthodoxy in practice, and the way in which it builds a hybrid legal order with consistent and, as we will see, decisive Tūhoe participation. Te Urewera exposes latent possibilities that were simply not visible in other cases, and it does so precisely because it thinks everything anew. It's worth following that journey.

Te Urewera: Adventures in Ontology

The most important contextual background for understanding the legal personality of Te Urewera are the Treaty negotiations between Māori groups and the New Zealand government. As Sanders (2018) explains, 'the grant of legal personality to Te Urewera and the Whanganui river took place as part of the Treaty of Waitangi settlement process, through which the Crown acknowledges breaches of its obligations to Māori under the 1840 agreement'. To understand the importance of the Treaty settlement process, it is necessary to briefly reflect on the history of New Zealand's colonization.

The first significant contact between Europeans and Māori dates back to 1769,[4] when the *Endeavour*, captained by James Cook, landed on the eastern shores of the North Island. Seventy years and many missionaries and settlers later, the British Crown and many (but not all) Māori chiefs signed the 1840 Treaty of Waitangi, the most important document in New Zealand's history (Jones 2016). After the signing in Waitangi, the Treaty was taken across the island for additional signatures. Tūhoe, the inhabitants of Te Urewera, have

4 Technically the first known contact with Europeans was 13 December 1642, when Abel Tasman sailed past New Zealand. However, this encounter did not lead to landing or settlement, which did not occur until Cook's arrival.

never signed,[5] though this does not mean that they, and their land, were not affected by this monumental event.

Indeed, starting in the 1860s, a period of aggressive colonization began, with land purchases and confiscations greatly expanding the settler populations. Demography shifted from Māori majority to Māori minority in little more than 50 years. The Māori population 'dropped from around [200,000] in 1840 to [40,000] in 1900. Epidemics of influenza, measles, diphtheria, and tuberculosis, as well as ill-health caused by changes in diet and living conditions, all affected the population. Other deaths, of course, occurred in battle with the colonizer ...' (Jackson 1992, 2). Te Urewera remained the last bastion of Māori *tikanga*,[6] as it was only in 1865 that the Crown 'confiscated much of [Tūhoe's] most productive land'.[7] Between 1865 and 1871 there was a war between the Crown and Tūhoe in Te Urewera which, by the Crown's own admission, devastated Māori groups through starvation, executions, and further appropriation of lands (O'Malley 2014, Finlayson 2014).

The Treaty of Waitangi was signed in two language versions, a Māori and an English one. The history of the difference between these two is extremely important and has been amply debated. One of the most contentious concepts for the purposes of the present discussion is that of *tino rangatiratanga*. Jones (2016, 54) explains that the term varies in meaning from 'self-government' to 'sovereignty' or 'full authority'. The Waitangi Tribunal has argued that 'no one

5 Ngai Tūhoe Deed of Settlement Summary (June 4, 2013). Also see Binney (2009).

6 Meaning law, way or custom. In legal discussions, the term is used to denote Māori law, that is to say legal custom of Māori origins and application. Much in the discussion of legal personality for nature centers around the idea that this construct represents a hybridization of *tikanga* Māori and Crown law. The word is composed of *tika*, meaning right or correct, and *nga*, which is the plural definitive article in te reo, the Māori language. *Tikanga* therefore indicates the right way of doing things, which brings it into much closer communication with the European tradition of natural law and natural rights than with the modern tradition of liberal individual rights.

7 Deed of Settlement Summary.

single English concept effectively captures the full meaning of the term' in part because, unlike sovereignty in English, it has spiritual connotations as well as implications of dominion over particular territories (Jones 2016, 56). In the Māori version, Article two of the Treaty of Waitangi guarantees the chiefs *tino rangatiratanga*. This term already opens up towards the vast and rich Māori *tikanga* that was slowly forced into the molds of state law.

Recent scholarship on the Treaty as well as recent judicial decisions have more or less settled on the opinion that, at the time of signing, the chiefs did not cede their sovereign ability to direct the life of the community or ownership of their lands (Sanders 2018, Jackson 1992). In the English version of Article One of the Treaty, 'sovereignty' was ceded to the Crown, while in the Māori version it was *kawanatanga*, or 'governorship' (Erueti 2017, 717). English colonists and their successive governments increasingly acted as if the Treaty of Waitangi had transferred sovereignty of Aotearoa to the Crown, while Māori chiefs operated under the understanding that they had retained *tino rangatiratanga*. Tūhoe have been remarkably consistent throughout this history in affirming *mana motuhake*, a term very close in meaning to *tino rangatiratanga*. As Higgins (2018, 130) explains, 'distinctions between *mana motuhake* and *tino rangatiratanga* are contextual rather than categorical, but while they have much in common, *mana motuhake* more strongly emphasizes independence from state and Crown and implies a measure of defiance'. This is not surprising given the especially conflictual history between Tūhoe and the Crown.

Throughout the 19th century, Tūhoe defiance was also expressed through the sheltering of other Māori people that were fleeing persecution elsewhere (Binney 2009), such that 'Richard Boast describes Te Urewera as the last "major bastion of Māori de-facto autonomy"' Higgins (2018, 130). This autonomy was officially recognized in law when, in 1896, 'the Urewera District Native Reserve Act provided for local Tūhoe self-government over a 656,000-acre Reserve, and for decisions about the use of land to be made collectively and according to Tūhoe custom. The Act guaranteed the protection of Tūhoe lands, which could not be sold without Tūhoe consent and then only to the Crown' (Finlayson 2014).

The Act was never implemented, though it set a unique precedent in recognizing Tūhoe's authority in Te Urewera. 'Perhaps the most remarkable aspect of [the Act] was its intention to give effect to tino rangatiratanga or mana motuhake' (Jones 2014). Despite this intention, the early 20th century saw blatant disregard for the Act, with 'the government simply… buying land interests directly from individuals, in direct contravention of its own laws' (O'Malley 2014). As if to catch up with the reality on the ground, in 1922 the government repealed the Urewera District Native Reserve Act, putting an end to this early period of experimentation in plural sovereignty. Further shrinkage of Tūhoe land ensued, which led to massive emigration from the area. In 1954, Te Urewera became a national park, which seemed to seal its fate as a settler fantasy of nature forever stolen from within an intricate human-nature genealogy.

It is significant to note the clear role of the national park designation in appropriating lands from Tūhoe authority. This was not a fluke of history or a unique event. Rather, nature conservation under the model of the national park has functioned as a system of enclosure and extension of state power since its inception in the United States (see Duffy et al 2019, Büscher et al 2012, Büscher and Fletcher 2020, Tănăsescu and Constantinescu 2020, Constantinescu and Tănăsescu 2018), where it was applied to native territories before being exported throughout the world together with colonial power. In the 20th century, nature conservation gave a new life to policies of territorial enclosure by providing the moral justification of environmental benefits. As Macpherson (2021b) recalls, Te Urewera "was declared a national park" and "'a jewel in the national conservation estate', without consultation with Tūhoe nor recognition that they had any special interest in the land".

This history of drowning out *tikanga* in favor of state law was most significantly affected by the Treaty of Waitangi Act of 1975, which inaugurated the Waitangi Tribunal, 'a standing commission of inquiry established to inquire into Māori claims that laws, policies, acts or omissions of the Crown are or were inconsistent with the principles of the Treaty of Waitangi' (Sanders 2018, 208). The Tribunal only has powers of recommendation, though this has not rendered it powerless. Indeed, 'the tribunal began to have an influence on public policy, despite its lack of powers to compel the government to take notice of its recommendations' (Belgrave 2013). As Belgrave continues, 'it was partly in recognition of this success that in 1985 the fourth Labour Government extended the tribunal's jurisdiction back to 1840, with far-reaching consequences that were only dimly understood at the time'. This set in motion the contemporary era of negotiations between the government and Māori *iwi* and *hapū* for breaches of the Treaty.[8]

The grant of legal personality to diverse landscapes in New Zealand should therefore be understood in the post-1985 context of Treaty settlements. It is this historical period that elevates the Treaty of Waitangi to the most significant document in Māori – Crown relations. Before 1985, the Treaty of Waitangi had no particular legal status or force. As Belgrave notes, 'until the creation of the Waitangi Tribunal, no court or commission of inquiry had needed to define what was actually agreed to at Waitangi' (Belgrave 2013). The idea that Māori-Crown relations are defined by the differences in translation briefly summarized above is itself a late 20th century narrative that accords well with the contemporary period of Treaty settlements. It also shows that the Treaty, in the 19th century, 'could not be pinned down to a single interpretation for its European participants, let alone among the more than 500 rangatira representing diverse Māori communities' (Belgrave 2013).

Tūhoe claims to Te Urewera, like *Whanganui iwi* claims to the Whanganui river, can be interpreted as complex negotiations about who owns the land, or more precisely about who has ultimate authority in governing the lands. The idea of legal personality provides a provisional solution to this question. Unlike in the cases explored in the previous chapter, we are here starting to see a specific context of contestation that, for largely pragmatic reasons, settles on the idea of legal personality as a possible negotiation tool. The issue of rights, as well as the idea of Nature, are much less prominent than the issues of ownership and authority (Sanders 2018, Macpherson 2019, 2021).

---

8 Names for Indigenous Māori descent groups. *Iwi* denotes a larger group than *hapū*.

The history of Treaty negotiations might suggest that Māori descent groups feature as fully equal participants in a process of negotiation. However, such Treaty negotiations always take place against a backdrop of state power to impose the general framework for discussion. Higgins makes the point that Treaty negotiations force Māori to come together in ways that are not based on Māori custom. She argues that 'the process that is placed upon iwi to create "mandated large natural groupings" by the Office of Treaty Settlements' is itself an imposed framework (Higgins 2019, 132). She continues: '…the settlement systems are not determined by Māori and often contravene *tikanga Māori*, or any "customary system of authority"'. This has the potential to create tensions within Māori communities, as *tikanga* systems of membership might or might not correspond with official requirements for commencing negotiations. In the case of Te Urewera, it was Te Kotahi a Tūhoe that received the mandate to negotiate with the Crown for Treaty settlements.[9]

Negotiations between Tūhoe representatives and the Crown began in 2005. For Tūhoe, the return of Te Urewera under their authority was non-negotiable, although it was far from clear at the outset what this return might look like. The government, in turn, feared that 'negotiating Te Urewera and mana motuhake would lead to Tūhoe creating a separate nation and closing borders and access to Te Urewera, which was still a National Park at the time. This sensationalism led to the Prime Minister removing Te Urewera from the negotiation table at the eleventh hour before the signing of the Agreement in Principle between the Crown and Tūhoe' (Higgins 2019, 135). This led to the halting of negotiations in 2010, because for Tūhoe 'Te Urewera and mana motuhake are inextricably linked'. The refusal to negotiate further on the part of Tāmati Kruger, Tūhoe chief negotiator and senior leader of Te Kotahi a Tūhoe, forced the

9 Echoing Higgins' point about the tensions that might be created by the requirement of a unified *iwi*, Binney recalls the internal struggles between *hapū* regarding who was the rightful representative of Te Urewera in negotiations with the Crown. See J. Binney, *Stories Without End: Essays 1975-2010* (Bridget Williams Books, 2010), pp. 364-5.

government back to the table and eventually resulted in the government granting legal entity status to Te Urewera.

Te Urewera Act 2014 establishes Te Urewera as a *legal entity*, a term used fairly consistently throughout the document. As I argued in Chapter 2, the idea of a legal person mixes moral and legal conceptions in ways that are not always helpful. Here, the idea of a legal entity offers a way out of the moral/legal confusion promoted by legal persons.[10] Te Urewera is not a person, first and foremost in Māori views. Rather, the legal compromise reached through negotiation institutes a new entity, a term that allows for a lot of openness as to how to conceive of what has been inaugurated. That being said, the text of Te Urewera Act also sometimes uses the two terms synonymously. For example, Section 11.1 declares that 'Te Urewera is a legal entity, and has all the rights, powers, duties, and liabilities of a legal person'. This reflects the undertheorized nature of the difference between legal entities and persons.

Section 11.2 mandates that the aforementioned rights, powers and duties must be exercised on behalf of Te Urewera by Te Urewera Board, therefore designating a specific representative for the legal entity. Constructing Te Urewera as an entity can therefore be interpreted as a way of being transparent about the artificiality of the construction itself, thereby allowing the Board ample discretion regarding how to represent Te Urewera and its specific life-form. Unlike the cases we saw previously, here the issue of standing is decided in a very specific way, i.e. by vesting it in the Board. I will come back to the significance of this.

The construction of Te Urewera as a legal entity in the context of the Treaty negotiations is a compromise that avoids vesting land ownership either in Tūhoe or the government. It also avoids vesting full political authority in either party and instead opts for the construction of a Board that would be the de facto and de jure governor of Te Urewera, while the owner is Te Urewera itself. Indeed, Section 17 states that the board was 'created in order to act on behalf of, and to "provide governance"' to Te Urewera. Subsequent sec-

---

10 See Tănăsescu (2020) for a detailed discussion of this point, in relation to both Te Urewera and the Ecuadorian constitution.

tions explicitly allow the Board to govern according to Tūhoe principles.[11] Tūhoe leaders have used the space opened up by the difference between 'providing governance' and 'Tūhoe principles': instead of opting for a conventional governance regime where people manage nature, Tūhoe ontology subverts the requirement of governance by recognizing natural entities themselves as capable of self-governance. This space of innovation is granted explicit approval by the law's designation of Te Urewera as an entity and therefore not modelled on pre-existing governance arrangements.

As Macpherson (2021b) points out, Te Urewera Act has precedents in New Zealand history inasmuch as it is similar to co-management agreements that the Crown had reached in the past with other *iwi*. However, the legal entity status is a clear departure, and one that comes out of Tūhoe insistence on negotiating common values on which the new arrangement could be based. Equally important is the fact that Tūhoe activism in this case cut its own path, adapted to specific historical and environmental conditions. The point of this arrangement, unlike other co-management ones, is to foreground the issues of ownership and authority, which are directly related to historical Tūhoe grievances.

In this context of ontological mixing between the Crown and Tūhoe, the rules for appointing Board members and the internal rules of decision making become very important for understanding how legal recognition might work in practice. Also important is the appointment panel, which consists of the trustees of Tūhoe Te Uru Taumatua,[12] the Minister of Conservation and the Minister of Treaty Negotiations. In the first three years of functioning, the Board is composed of four representatives for both the Crown and Tūhoe. After the first three years of functioning, this changes to six

11 18.2 and 18.3.

12 The seven trustees are available here: https://www.ngaituhoe.iwi.nz/governance.

members appointed by Tūhoe and three by the Ministers.[13] The appointment panel can remove previously appointed Board members.

Section 31 establishes that 'Board members must promote unanimous or consensus decision making, as the context requires'. Sections 33 and onwards lay down the various decision rules. If a decision cannot be reached by consensus and must be put to a vote, it must be carried by an 80% majority of those present and at least two members who were appointed by the Ministers. Section 40 declares that 'financially speaking and for tax purposes, Te Urewera and the Board are the same person'.

These kinds of details are important because it is only through them that the novelty of this arrangement can be recognized. It is also through the particularities of the case that we can start to see that here we are really talking about a new *political* arrangement, over and beyond the legal innovation. The very point of the legal innovation is to create ongoing debates about a new and underdefined actor. The lack of precise definition *is* the point, and taken together with the obligation to govern in constant dialogue among parties (natural ones included) it forces a constant reassessment of all actors. In this sense, Te Urewera act offers the possibility of understanding all parties involved in novel ways, because it does not set the idea of personhood as a model to be emulated. Instead, it focuses on the governance arrangement that realigns power relations away from Crown dominance and towards an as yet unknown future.

According to the 2014 Act, the Board is tasked with drafting and following a management plan, Te Kawa o Te Urewera.[14] The language that characterizes future management plans in the Te Urewera Act falls squarely within a Western legal and managerial tradition dominated by outcomes, targets, and so on. As Carwyn Jones (2016) points out, Māori terms are heavily used in the preamble and

---

13 At the time of this writing, the second Board had commenced its term. In addition to Board members, the Te Urewera Act 2014 appoints a Tūhoe chairman in perpetuity.

14 Hereafter Te Kawa. Available at https://www.ngaituhoe.iwi.nz/te-kawa-o-te-urewera.

historical parts of the documents (the symbolic ones), while there is "a general paucity of Māori language within the operational provisions of these instruments". This experience was very similar to the ones of Ecuador and Bolivia, where indigenous notions are heavily used in the preamble and overall the symbolic parts of the text.

However, the Board brilliantly subverts state power through the management plan itself. Crucially, this kind of subversion was already made possible by the careful and long-term parsing out of power relations, something that was not explicitly done in Ecuador and Bolivia. It is, after all, the law itself that allows full freedom of drafting a plan, which opens up spaces of authority that can further consolidate Tūhoe control. One purpose of the management plan, as explained by the law, is 'to set objectives and policies for Te Urewera'. Te Kawa was drafted with strong input from Tāmati Kruger, a chief negotiator and senior leader of Te Kotahi a Tūhoe, as well as Board member and chairman of Tūhoe Te Uru Taumatua, who had been instrumental in negotiating the 2014 Act with the Crown. He turned the conventional framing of the relation between nature and management on its head by stating that 'Te Kawa is about the management of people for the benefit of the land – it is not about land management'.

Even though the 2014 Act stays broadly within the apparatus of the State, Tūhoe managed to create a space where their authority could become fuller. They did this in several ways. First, and perhaps most importantly, through the direct linking of Te Urewera to a designated representative, namely the Board. Unlike in the other cases we saw so far, here there was no assumption of rights doing their work by themselves, as it were. Tūhoe were acutely aware of the need to have their own relationship to the land recognized as primary. This leads Macpherson (2021b) to conclude that Te Urewera act, if seen from the anthropocentric – ecocentric distinction, is squarely within the first camp. She argues, correctly in my view, that Te Urewera can be just as well seen as an indigenous rights case, rather than a rights of nature case that follows the theoretical history explored earlier. This means that Te Urewera shows a path for the rights of nature that goes through careful political arrangements and dismisses altogether the notion that the law can, or even has to be, ecocentric.

Second, the concept of legal entity, hitched to the representative power that Tūhoe secured for themselves, allows them broad margins in defining how the land will be governed. These margins had to be secured precisely because the terms of the negotiation themselves were imposed by the settler state. In other words, Tūhoe could only sediment their authority in Te Urewera through a legal mechanism that would allow them to define what authority may mean in practice. All of the detailed provisions of the act set up an infrastructure for the deployment of authority, guided by shared values. But the actual content of Tūhoe government is to be decided in practice, partly because it is through practice that it *can* be defined. This is a powerful rejection of totality thinking.

Lastly, Te Kawa steers clear of the issue of rights altogether. Te Urewera will have some rights because of its legal entity status (Macpherson 2019), but what these may be is nowhere defined. This way, the historical baggage that comes with the concept of rights is cut out altogether. Instead, the management plan focuses on reciprocity with the land and the responsibility people have towards it (Tănăsescu 2022). Though rights have become hegemonic to the point of saturation, this arrangement shows how to side-step their totalizing power and propose alternatives that may as well, in the long run, erode some of that power.

The issue of nature conservation is mostly vested in the Board and therefore left open. When it was a national park, Te Urewera was managed by the Department of Conservation which, under the current arrangement, lost control of its former 'crown jewel'. In fact, there is nothing particularly 'environmental' about the construction of Te Urewera as a legal entity. Macpherson (2021b) points out that the powers given to the Board include those of creating bylaws and "to authorize certain activities that are otherwise prohibited under conservation laws, including the taking, cutting or destroying of indigenous lands and the hunting of indigenous animals".

This is because Tūhoe, like many other Indigenous Nations elsewhere, relate to the environment through a mode of paying attention to it that is reproduced through use. The Tūhoe concept of management is *mana me mauri*, that is to say the "sensitive perception of spiritual and living force in a place" (Macpherson 2021b). But this kind of perception can only occur with repeated interactions that partly, and importantly, center on *using* existing resources. The conservation ethic, which relegated Indigenous People to noble guardians of nature, is again revealed as an imposition.

The provisions of Te Urewera Act were not primarily motivated by environmental concerns, but rather by power relations. The rights of nature appeared as a pragmatic way of solving a dispute, and it was used creatively to this end. As far as the state is concerned, the settlement reached with Tūhoe is final. However, given the history of colonial relations, there is no reason to believe that this is in fact so. The new legal provisions in Te Urewera are but the next stage in a centuries-old dispute over how to govern, and who has the right to do so. It remains to be seen how this history of Crown – Tūhoe interactions will develop under the new conditions inaugurated by the Act.

To be clear, Te Urewera Act is not a piece of legislation that recognizes Tūhoe self-determination as such. Settler states would sooner accept self-owning land than Indigenous owned one, which would threaten the very definition of a state as wielding homogenous power over a homogenous territory. The self-ownership of Te Urewera also comes very close to corporate personhood, which further makes it available for integration within already existing legal infrastructures.

The exact way in which authority will be exercised by the board is unclear, for several reasons. First, Te Urewera is not one thing, but rather a contested space *within* Tūhoe communities. From afar, it looks as if Tūhoe are a homogenous and united group, but inasmuch as Indigenous agency and multiplicity is truly recognized, it stands to reason that there are internal politics as well. Second, the concession of authority by the Crown is partial because some areas are still designated 'wilderness areas', signaling the unwillingness of the state to fully let go of its history of conservation. Though the management of such areas needs to be done in consultation with the board, this is not really full recognition of Indigenous autonomy.

Lastly, the board is tasked with undertaking measures that have everything to do with how the state conducts its business of governing. In particular, it is tasked with giving permits for a multitude of activities, some of which come under traditional use. The representative of Te Urewera is therefore tasked with bureaucratizing its functioning, an aspect that may well lead to frustration and contestation within Tūhoe communities.

This notwithstanding, new ground for more Tūhoe autonomy is being prepared, particularly through Te Kawa, the management plan. To even call this document a 'management plan' is deceiving, as that name comes with a particular concept of targets, top-down assessments, human control, and so on, which the law in fact mandates. It also comes with the idea of guardianship, which has been ubiquitous in the coverage of the New Zealand cases. However, the Board is *not* the guardian of Te Urewera, but its representative. Te Kawa makes sure that this point is immediately clear by announcing its intention to manage people, not the land.

The Western idea of guardianship is not the only concept Te Kawa rejects. Indeed, the concept of Nature that we saw earlier is also rejected for the radically emplaced Te Urewera, which is characterized as a special *marae*, that is to say a community house where vital issues are discussed and ancestors met (see Kawharu 2010). Te Kawa states that Te Urewera has its own way of being and further disrupts the colonial making of Indigenous People as inherent guardians by proposing that the character of Te Urewera needs to be constantly rediscovered, as Tūhoe need to themselves reinvent their own traditions. The latest Annual Plan available (2020-2021) announces quite boldly that Tūhoe are out of practice in their own ancestral ways, precisely because of colonialism. They therefore need to relearn ways of being that are free from the colonial inheritance touching everyone and everything. The process of relearning is always a part of the cultural hygiene of a people: constant reiteration and gradual change *is* the way in which traditions are perpetually reinvented.

The issue of rights is nowhere present in Te Kawa. Instead, it is all about the responsibility that people have to relearn ways of being in the world that are true to the particularities of a place. All of this does not mean that Te Urewera is a model to follow everywhere; drawing that conclusion would bring us right back to the universalist discourse of rights of nature that I find so problematic. The difference between Te Urewera Act and Te Kawa lends support to Jones' argument that the Act does not sufficiently recognize Tūhoe tikanga. If it did, there would be no need for such a major departure, in the management plan, from many of its provisions.

This notwithstanding, Te Urewera shows a way of using legal entity status as a potential tool of empowerment, while acknowledging its limitations. It also shows how the rights of nature are not automatically about 'the environment' and that they need not be fixated on rights or a general concept of Nature. Rights can be a useful tool, given certain contexts, but the context is everything. Even in New Zealand, where countless Treaty settlement claims have been lodged, only a small number of them settled on rights of nature as a partial solution. I want to now turn to another one of those.

Whanganui River and its Human Face

In 2017, Te Awa Tupua Act was signed into law. The claims settlement history that was recounted in the previous section also largely applies to this case, though of course the particular interactions between Whanganui iwi and the Crown were different than those between Tūhoe and the Crown. That being said, the 2017 legislation offering legal recognition to Whanganui river came out of the same process of claims settlement. Throughout the history of colonization, Whanganui iwi had also been remarkably consistent in claiming that Crown activities in the river contravened iwi authority, which they had never given up.

Te Awa Tupua[15] is defined by the act in line with Māori ontology as an "indivisible and living whole, comprising the Whanganui river from the mountains to the sea, incorporating all its physical and metaphysical elements" (Art.12). Of course, the separation between physical and metaphysical is itself a settler way of understanding

15 This is the name of the river in Te Reo Māori, the Māori language.

Māori thought, a by now instinctive attempt to save the idea that there is but one world with different views on it. For Māori, however, Te Awa is an ancestor, a powerful being whose separation into riverbed, water, tributaries, and so on, they have always opposed.

The Act affords Te Awa the status of "legal person", potentially wading straight into the legal/moral thicket already explored. Crucially, it also designates one representative for Te Awa, namely Te Pou Tupua, the equivalent of Te Urewera's Board, here described as the "human face" of the river. Predictably, international coverage of this case has both assimilated it to rights of nature elsewhere, as if it was part of the same seamless history, and presented Whanganui iwi as the guardians of the river. Neither of these claims are true. This legislation shows once again the diversity of ways of thinking about the role of the law in human emplacement.

Let's take a closer look, for instance, at the issue of guardianship. I suspect that its persistence has to do with the ecotheological history that specifically theorizes human's highest role in nature as one of guardianship (Chapter 2). This also corresponds to the neat idea of an expanding circle of moral concern: when humans are finally the conscious guardians of nature, the circle would have expanded all the way. The idea of guardianship construed thus also works very well with the formatting of Indigenous People as belonging, by nature, to a specific place. There is a seeming paradox here: on the one hand, human history is seen as a continuous expansion of moral concern, while those that supposedly are already acting as guardians (the Indigenous) are precisely the people that are not modern and therefore supposedly steeped in pre-expansion morality.

The paradox is resolved by realizing, as I have previously argued, that this image of the Indigenous as natural guardians is a Western construction. Once again, this does not mean that Indigenous Peoples are inherently destructive. It simply means that no human group is naturally benign, unless it is denied its own history and agency by more powerful human groups. In order to dispel some of the fog created by this contradictory idea of guardianship and its association with expanding moral consciousness, it helps to attend more closely to how Māori thinking, in this case, construed 'guardianship'.

Anne Salmond, Aotearoa New Zealand's foremost anthropologist, recounts how Māori thought conceives of guardians as *taniwha*, that is to say local spirits, usually in the form of animals that take care of a particular place and are a gauge of its well-being. The Māori term usually translated as guardian is *kaitiaki*, whereas *kaitiakitanga* translates as guardianship. As the Waitangi Tribunal Freshwater stage two report explains, "traditionally, there were certain creatures, taniwha or birds, which were kaitiaki and 'invested with the spirits of ancestors or closely related to remote ancestors by whakapapa [genealogy]'" (p.118). The report continues by mentioning the important detail that "the observation of those kaitiaki by the people revealed whether 'all is well in the world or whether some action is needed'". People, then, are *observers* of kaitiaki, not themselves guardians of a place. Human beings exist as such only inasmuch as they are members of genealogical networks (*whakapapa*) that transmit certain responsibilities from generation to generation. And one such responsibility is that of careful observation of a place, in order to respect its *mauri* (life-force) and *hau* (spirit or vitality).

Māori tradition is as changeable as any other, but it is important to set out the broad conceptual outline of a completely different world, not just another 'cultural' point of view on the same material world. For Māori, places are not dumb matter, but are charged with ancestral power that has its own logic within which human beings have to fit themselves. When the vitality of a place is affected, then humans can intervene in ways that try to uphold the power of non-human kaitiaki. What this may mean in practice is entirely context-dependent, but part of that context, for the last centuries, has been the need for Māori to translate their concepts into Western language. Despite the adoption of the concept of legal personality, for example, it is nonetheless remarkable how consistent the resistance to the Western concept of guardianship has been.

Equally consistent has been Māori insistence on the need to *use* the environment in specific kinds of ways while not using it in others. In the case of water, for example, Māori tradition forbids the discharge of any waste into water bodies, or the fusing of initially separate waterways (though it also considers 'a river' to be formed by the whole catchment). It similarly relegates different activities (swimming, washing, drinking) to different areas of the river, such that the *mauri* of the river, and therefore the strength of its *kaitiaki*, are not affected. But Māori rules dictating interactions with, in this case, a river, are there in order to propagate a certain indefinite use of water. And whereas humans have the power to destroy through incorrect action, they do not have the same power to restore, precisely because they were not guardians to begin with, but mere users.

In the case of Whanganui river, Te Pou Tupua is defined as its human face, its representative perhaps, precisely because it cannot be, under Māori ontology, its guardian. "The purpose of Te Pou Tupua", the law states, "is to be the human face of Te Awa Tupua and act in the name of Te Awa Tupua" (Art. 18.2). It is important to stress that the idea of a human face is a compromise as well, an ontological hybrid, but one that veers closer to Māori ontology than the idea of guardianship does. Schedule 8 of the Act, for example, explicitly recognizes the existence of specific place-based relations between *hapū* and at least 240 rapids (*ripo*) that exist along the river. "Each ripo", the document states, "is inhabited by a kaitiaki (spiritual guardian), which is particular to each hapū". Notice that the word guardian is only ever used in relation to non-human kaitiaki. Also of great significance is the fact that the law, precisely under Māori influence, finds it necessary to locate itself at an ontological level that is quite uncomfortable for it: the level of places within the river network and the level of the privileged relationships that hold between people and these places.

The role of people is therefore one of *collective* responsibility "for maintaining the mauri of the ripo and, in so doing, the collective mauri of Te Awa Tupua" (p.88). This maintenance, which is a collective responsibility, is achieved by paying close attention to the non-human guardians of various places, because it is the "kaitiaki of the ripo [that] provide insight, guidance, and premonition in relation to matters affecting the Whanganui river, its resources and life in general". The issue of paying attention surfaces here as well as in

Te Urewera, particularly in its management plan that gave voice to Tūhoe ontology more fully than the Act itself. The idea of attention underlines that, in relational ways of thinking (as opposed to the modern binary ones), one is always already grounded in *some* place. To know that place is to use it in certain kinds of ways that are legitimated by one's ability to pay attention to natural cycles and their changeable rhythms.

These parts of the legislation, which are clearly highly influenced by Māori legal and philosophical traditions, do not shy away from using the concept of resource, partly because use, unlike in the ecotheological history I have explored, is not frowned upon as such. In fact, the particularities of each place are in part known through the varied uses that they make possible. "Each ripo has unique physical characteristics and is valued accordingly". Part of the valuation is given by the traditions that put those characteristics to human use, for example by adapting fishing techniques to each place. That kind of place-based knowledge has survived, and this legislation attempts to bring those 'informal' legal traditions into codified versions that would allow for a more autonomous interaction with the settler state that is there to stay.

Because this agreement, like in the case of Te Urewera before, was based on the particularities of the New Zealand context, legal personality appears in a form that the earlier theory of rights for nature could not have predicted nor facilitated. Here, legal personality is not primarily concerned with rights, nor with inserting itself within binary oppositions of the thing/property or nature/resource kind. All of the oppositions we explored earlier are simply sidestepped, and legal personality is made to do something that theory did not yet know it could do. The legal personality of Te Awa Tupua attempts to solve a problem of authority over particular lands, and it is precisely its highly open nature (it has no particular content) that allows for the ontological and legal hybridization on display.

This is best seen through the political apparatus that the law mandates such that the human face of the river (Te Pou Tupua) can do its work of speaking on behalf of Te Awa Tupua. It is there, in the details of those arrangements, that the truly revolutionary nature of the New Zealand cases is most visible. The 2017 law does not simply grant standing to Te Pou Tupua and leave it at that. Instead, it inaugurates a highly complex and entirely novel arrangement that ensures that the human face of the river speaks in democratic fashion and acts deliberatively. This is another example of hybridization at work. Neither Māori tradition nor the settler one were particularly preoccupied in the past with democratic principles. But under present conditions, the only legitimate way in which Te Pou Tupua can act is in highly consultative fashion. The apparatus that makes that possible, however, had to be invented.

For example, Te Pou Tupua is to perform "landowner functions" on behalf of Te Awa Tupua (19.1(d)). This, as in the case of Te Urewera, means that the river owns itself, but that the landlord is yet another element, namely its human face. The appointment rules for who can be member of Te Pou Tupua (20) further make it clear that this is an unprecedented figure, and especially a new kind of political figure fit for a settler world whose right to be there in the first place cannot be effectively questioned. By law, Te Pou Tupua has to encompass both Crown and Iwi representatives, in effect claiming the right to represent the river as a shared duty for old rivals.

This is not all. Te Pou Tupua cannot simply decide what is in the best interest of the river, even though it is itself a deliberative institution. Instead, the law mandates that it relies on Te Karewao, meaning a group of advice providers, and Te Kōpuka (29ff), meaning "a permanent joint committee" (33.1). The purpose of all of these different institutions is to safeguard the well-being of Te Awa Tupua. To do this, Te Kōpuka has the specific function of drafting Te Heke Ngahuru (a long-term strategy or plan for the river; its purpose is spelled out in 35). Finally, there are four principles (Tupua Te Kawa, 13a-d) that the strategy drafted by Te Kōpuka and implemented by Te Pou Tupua with the advice of Te Karewao is to be based on. These principles affirm the inalienable relationship between all aspects of the river (creaturely, geomorphological, spiritual, and so on).

This arrangement seems very complicated, and it is. The joint committee, for example, may consist of no more than 17 members, and each must be appointed according to certain rules. Everything, including who counts as iwi and hapū, is highly regulated. All in all, this amounts to a new governance framework that is not at all about rights, nor about Nature, nor about guardianship, but about ways of carving out political power in relation to beings that have until now only been part of Māori worlds. The membership of Te Kōpuka is the most telling, as it reunites all actors with some sort of interest in the river, from tourism to resource extraction to the operator of the hydroelectric powerplant already in operation. Nature conservation appears as just another interest, with one representative only. The life of the river in the 21st century, clearly, cannot be thought of in the dualist terms of the settler tradition, nor in Māori terms alone. This Act, together with Te Urewera, are the most detailed and painstaking hybrid arrangement to make use of legal personality to date.

Whether the framework set up in this case will work, and what that may even mean, is to be seen in the long duration of history. Māori know this and do not seem to be under pressure to 'deliver' immediate results, precisely because what may count as a good outcome is entirely up to the durability of the deliberative process inaugurated through the Act. The temporal dimension of the case is very significant, because it is itself based on the rhythms of the surrounding world. It would be absurd to mandate that within a matter of months a centennial history, and the infinitely longer lifetime of the river, would be brought into line by a piece of legislation. Paying close attention to the *time* of the environment imposes a long duration to the legislative apparatus itself. Te Urewera follows the same temporal patience. In its online communication, the board is very careful to stress that results will be seen in time, because the time of the land is what dictates relationships with it.

There is no denying the difficulty of the framework involved in this case and the highly ambiguous nature of what success may mean. From the point of view of the rights of nature, I think that these cases can already be counted as successes, if nothing else because they reveal possibilities inherent in legal personality that were simply absent in the theory. They also demystify the relationship between rights and indigeneity in ways that are extremely helpful going forward. Finally, they show how ontological hybridization may happen without dictating either why it must happen or its precise content. In other words, Te Urewera and Te Awa Tupua show how far the law can be pushed and how to bridge the unavoidable generality of Western law with the place-based philosophical traditions that, despite centuries of violent colonialism, still endure.

Chapter V: The Perils of Totality
A Short Foray into Modernist Thought

So far, I have analyzed two different kinds of cases of rights of nature. On the one hand, I discussed cases that have explicitly drawn from a theoretical tradition steeped in what I have called ecotheology. On the other hand, I have also presented two cases (Te Urewera and Te Awa Tupua) that have used the concept of legal personality in radically different ways. These are very important for future rights theory, as they have revealed previously hidden potential and inaugurated a different theoretical course, away from ecotheology. These two kinds of cases – ecotheological rights of existence and legal personality arrangements – are not, however, the only ones. In this chapter I want to look at several other instances, with the benefit of having the aforementioned cases in the background.

I will examine the legal personality of several different rivers and several different places, as well as the push to pass international rights for nature laws in one form or another. These cases combine elements of the ones explored so far, showing both the limits of typologies and the fluidity of nature's rights in practice. Atrato river in Colombia, the Amazon rainforest, two rivers in India, all rivers in Bangladesh, and a potential UN declaration of the Rights of Mother Earth are at different judicial levels, reached through different mechanisms, and in many other ways completely different from each other. These differences are important. But equally important is to recognize a certain intellectual inheritance that connects them.[1] Through mechanisms of policy diffusion (the formal and informal passing of policy ideas from one place to another), all of these cases inherit parts of ecotheology that combine in different ways with the kind of place-based thinking on display in Aotearoa New Zealand. They share many of the same intellectual assumptions seen in Ecuador and Bolivia, and therefore the same potential problems, even though they seem to be concerned with places.

The concepts of nature, rights, and guardianship are important junctions between rights of nature theory and practice. Another such conceptual connector is what I call 'totality'. We have seen it already at work in the ecotheological concept of Nature, as well as of 'humanity'. Totality, and the insistence on it, is a potent marker of modernist thinking, namely the kind of thought originating in Western Europe at the time of the Enlightenment that considers itself to be universal and therefore applicable everywhere and to everyone. It is the kind of thought that thinks in terms of "humanity" versus "nature", and that looks for essential qualities abstracted from any lived experience (also see Debaise 2017, Tănăsescu 2022). It is the thought that sees current ecological problems as the result of humanity going astray, instead of very specific forms of power gaining momentum because of the benefit to certain groups at the expense of others.

The reliance on totality is insidious precisely because modernity has all but saturated the landscape of thought and practice (Chakrabarty 2009b, 2018). Virtually no-one is opposed to "modern development", just as no-one can be opposed to rights. What I want to argue is that one of the reasons why rights are unopposable (or, to say it differently, hegemonic) is the same as why modern development appears unstoppable. Simply stated, moderns (mostly everyone today) have been trained to think in universal abstractions, and they do so even when supposedly opposing modern ills (like environmental destruction). The cases I will survey here exemplify the subversive power of totality. They also show why, in rights of nature theory and practice, we need much more than ecotheology in order

1 This inheritance is not limited to philosophical concepts, but also to conceptions of law.

to overcome modernist ecological predicaments and to be able to propose alternatives that are truly different.

One of the motivating questions of this analysis is whether the law can use mechanisms that are intrinsic parts of colonial enclosure and environmental destruction in order to oppose such depredations. These mechanisms are legal personality, rights, and – to an equally great extent – universality and totality. I don't propose to answer this question once and for all; that pretense would be absurd. But keeping the question central to the expansion of rights is crucial for the intellectual and moral development of this growing trend.

Many Landscapes, Some Places[2]

Atrato

Atrato river, in the department of Chocó, Colombia, became a legal person in 2016.[3] This grant of legal personality to a particular place was neither a municipal ordinance, nor a constitutional one

2 The following sections discuss cases in Colombia and India for which I undertook no independent field work. For the other cases discussed in this book, I did independent field work in the languages of the relevant countries. The language barrier, especially in the Indian case, should not be underestimated. Though I do not claim to have the final word on any cases, I think that more errors of interpretation may arise in the following sections, where I rely primarily on secondary sources by authors that may also not have had the opportunity to do independent research in the relevant languages. I have done my best to consult Colombian and Indian authors first and foremost, but I think that it is still necessary to contextualize my own research of these cases. In the Colombian case, I have consulted official documents in the original language.

3 The decision was only made public in May 2017. See Macpherson and Clavijo Ospina (2020). "Person" here translates the term "sujeto", which can also be translated as "subject". For the purposes of the argument, I treat both as synonymous.

(in the sense of being included in the constitution of the state), nor a national law, nor the result of claim settlement processes. Whereas until now I juxtaposed an ecotheological rights tradition to the place-based one, this case combines elements of both in surprising ways. In particular, it differs in how the idea of legal personality was reached.

Atrato river became a legal person out of judicial pronouncement. This means that the legal personality of Atrato was not reached as part of a more or less explicit political process. This does not mean that it doesn't have potentially enormous political consequences, but it is important to note that there is a whole class of cases under development (including the Ganga and Yamuna rivers, in India) that appear entirely out of judicial decisions (O'Donnell 2018). Judges, for reasons I will explore, have decided in these cases that the best way to protect the rivers (or places) under discussion was by proclaiming them to be legal persons.

The Colombian Constitutional Court recognized Atrato river as a subject of rights in 2016, while the Colombian Supreme Court did the same for the Colombian Amazon rainforest in 2018. Both of these cases demonstrate, as Calzadilla (2019, 3) argues, that "rights of nature/ecosystems can be recognized by both legislative and judicial channels". Though in the case of rights of nature theory strictly speaking this possibility was not explicitly formulated, it does nonetheless conform to the theoretical view of legal personality as something that is simply declared by a competent authority. Why that may be done, and to what end, remain questions to be explored. But *that* it can be done is beyond doubt.

In the Atrato case, the court proclaimed it a legal person in response to a *tutela* action brought by an NGO – *Tierra Digna* – on behalf of residents suffering the harm of illegal mining activities on the river. A tutela action is a constitutional mechanism that allows any person to "request any judge in the country to protect his/her fundamental constitutional rights when they are being violated by a state agent or an individual" (Calzadilla 2019, 4). Because of the high levels of pollution caused by mining activities on the river, the NGO used the tutela mechanism in order to compel the state to take protective action for safeguarding the wellbeing of local residents as well as that of the river.

Several things are important to note at the outset. First, this case begins as a violation of the rights *to* nature of the local residents (as well as a host of other human rights) and becomes – through the decision of the judge – a case of rights *for* nature. This is not the first time we encounter the tension between these two different kinds of rights. It again shows that the binary thinking in terms of anthropocentric versus ecocentric laws is not really fit for purpose: it cannot make sense of rights of nature laws themselves, which are supposedly ecocentric. As Macpherson and Clavijo Ospina (2020) argue, this kind of case raises doubts "about the usefulness of the ecocentric/anthropocentric divide".

Second, the mining activities that were the source of contention and harm were already illegal. In other words, the state already had mechanisms at its disposal to protect the wellbeing of local inhabitants, human and non-human alike. The Colombian Constitution itself, which made space for a tutela action, is also known as an *ecological constitution*. This point must be underlined because of the often-repeated advocacy claim that giving nature rights is necessary in order to ensure environmental protection. But no compelling reason is given for *why* these would fare better than already existing legislation, especially once we dispel the myth that ecocentrism can exist as such, let alone be effective in practice. In the end, the issue of state power is central and cannot be avoided. Chapter 6 will show how, in the cases of Ecuador and Bolivia extractive industries have *increased* since the passage of those country's radical-seeming rights of nature laws. This is a possibility that cannot be ignored in the Atrato case as well.

Similarly, the 2018 decision to grant the Amazon legal personality status came from another tutela action against government actors that failed to uphold resident's constitutional rights in the face of increasing deforestation. Just like in the Atrato case, this decision enacts a passage from the violation of rights to a healthy environment towards rights for the environment itself. Similarly, the deforestation under question was already illegal. Finally, the role of the state is ambiguous and central: In the Amazon case, the state was explicitly targeted as a cause of deforestation, while the idea of legal personality also depends on the state for its functioning. It may seem as if the mechanism of judicial decision sidesteps the importance of the state, but it does not: the newly created Atrato and Amazon legal entities will have to be incorporated within political processes mediated by and through the state; they cannot exist in the hands of judges alone nor, perhaps, should they.

In the Atrato case, the court gave the river specific rights, namely to "protection, conservation, maintenance and restoration" (operative part 4). These rights are very similar to the ones coming out of the ecotheological tradition analyzed in depth earlier, though here they are applied to a particular place. The right of restoration raises the same conundrums already explored, as by the admission of the court itself it is impossible to currently establish the 'original' course of the river (see Calzadilla 2019). The judicial decision in this case repeats the majority of ecotheological orthodoxy, from the gendered use of nature as feminine figure to the anthropocentric – ecocentric distinction and the idea that rights are recognized and depend on the existence of intrinsic values.

This case is both place-based in that legal personality applies to Atrato river, a particular being in a particular place, and is steeped in totality thinking. This combination is striking, and it remains to be seen just how it may play out in practice. But exposing conceptual commitments is already a good indicator of what may happen. The specific combination in this case is brought about by the international diffusion of the two kinds of rights of nature exemplified by Ecuador and Bolivia on the one hand and New Zealand on the other. But the lack of proper attention to their differences allows ecotheology and totality thinking to monopolize the way in which rights are conceived of and implemented, even when applied to specific territories.

For example, the court frames the legal personality of Atrato in terms of "the planet" and "humanity". It claims that "nature" must be recognized as an entity with intrinsic value, though it also speaks about the necessity to protect resources for future generations, in line with the sustainable development commitments already present in Colombia's ecological constitution. But under the premises of intrinsic value that the court itself upholds, why would future generations be allowed to use resources at all, on their own terms? This tension between intrinsic value and resource use is not a real tension, but one created by the theoretical artifact of framing the rights of nature as a passage from anthropocentrism to ecocentrism (as part of the expanding circle of moral concern). As I have argued in the case of Te Urewera and Te Awa Tupua, use as such is central to a-modern ways of living. In the neoliberal universe that ecotheological rights cannot but inhabit, there will always be an unresolvable tension between use and intrinsic values.

The majority of the literature starting to take stock of the Atrato and Amazon cases continues to frame these as a passage from anthropocentric to ecocentric law (with notable exceptions, such as Macpherson and Clavijo Ospina 2020). This is because of the so-far absent questioning of rights of nature orthodoxy. In fact, it is impossible for the rights of nature to be consistently ecocentric, and no case to date has managed this unmanageable feat. Besides the lack of consistency, there are two basic problems with thinking in terms of the opposition anthropo-eco: it repeats exactly the same opposition that is foundational for modernist ways of thinking and is therefore impotent to overcome these; and it depoliticizes rights by making it seem as if the problem of environmental degradation and destruction is nothing but a problem of having the wrong kind of consciousness (rooted in the 'anthropo-)'. This latter problem obscures the fundamental role of political infrastructures in *causing* environmental destruction, a thesis that has been amply demonstrated, beyond reasonable doubt, in the vast literature on political ecology. The underlying problem of environmental destruction is not the lack of ecocentric values, now widely shared, but rather the willful persistence of political arrangements that demand a consumptive relationship to the environing world for their own reproduction.

The irony of the anthropocentric – ecocentric framework is that it modernizes indigenous thinking, thus rendering it much less radical. Indigenous thinking is mostly of the relational type because it is not predicated on some foundational separation of humans from nature (Tănăsescu 2020, Macpherson 2021). The image of this separation in Biblical cultures is that of the fall, which is often repeated in rights of nature literature precisely because of the influence of ecotheology: man has fallen away from his Mother, and the fall is basically an error of thinking. Instead, indigenous philosophies have much more ambiguous genders for both the human and the natural side (they can contextually change; see last section for discussion in relation to Māori conceptions) and don't posit an original fall but an original differentiation into types of beings that, crucially, continue to have access to each other. The error of environmental destruction is therefore not primarily one of thinking, but one of *doing*, which is always a political error: a community member can only be destructive of the environment if the political infrastructure of her community allows it.

Indeed, the Chocó region through which Atrato flows is a densely layered landscape of historical uses that all have to do with various political infrastructures that make certain kinds of living, and doing, possible. The current population of the region is both overwhelmingly Indigenous and Afro-descendant, and overwhelmingly poor (the poorest in one of the most unequal countries in the world). This coincidence of poverty and ethnic background is no coincidence at all, but rather a trademark of settler states everywhere. The Afro-descendent community owes its very existence in this territory to the slave trade that captured the vast natural resources of this 'marginal' territory for transfer to the centers of power. In fact, artisanal mining has been a presence in the region (Atrato is rich in gold) since the 16th century (Macpherson and Clavijo Ospina 2020, Cagüeñas et al 2020). The 'traditional' panning for gold gave way to a mechanized and much more destructive form of mining in the 1990s. But it is important to see that at each step of interaction with the riverine environment, there is a political infrastructure that allows and makes possible certain activities, despite (and often because of) the law.

The anthropocentric - ecocentric framework is paradigmatically steeped into the modernist obsession with totality and grand narratives, a move that is anathema to highly localized ways of thinking and doing. The influence of totality thinking on the Colombian Constitutional Court is perhaps nowhere better seen than when the court identifies the human species itself as the main culprit for ecological devastation. It also thinks that its own action of declaring Atrato as a bearer of rights is part of a change in consciousness that is necessary for reorienting human behavior away from ecological sin and towards intrinsic value virtue.

These kinds of claims are not supposed to be verifiable or factual. Instead, to the extent that they have any meaning at all, it is because of the underlying theoretical construction that brings them forth. Humanity did not fall from Eden and lose its native benign ways. Instead, a well-documented history of colonial capitalism, which mutated into neoliberal consumerism actively promoted by nation states, has occasioned ecological crises (Tzouvala 2020). There is plenty of eco-consciousness to go around, but until the nation state is no longer predicated on neoliberal consumption, none of that will matter decisively. The 21st century miners devastating the poorest region of Colombia are part and parcel of a transnational network of resource extraction that the state makes possible and, on occasion, directly controls.

Besides receiving the status of legal person and a series of rights, Atrato was also granted guardians. This was an explicit reflection of the Whanganui case, though the nuance of Whanganui *iwi* being the human face of their river, and not its guardian, was lost. The way in which the Whanganui case has been appropriated by ecotheological rights influences the way in which policy diffuses from one place to another: the way laws from elsewhere are presented comes to influence new rights of nature cases (Kauffman and Martin 2017b). In this diffusion the work of the transnational network of rights of nature advocacy is undeniably strong. This is why it is crucial to restore the diversity of theoretical and practical orientations, so as to avoid a perpetuation of the same ecotheological tropes in myriad cases, together with their tensions and inconsistencies. These tensions are perhaps nowhere better exemplified than in the court's dealing with the idea of guardianship.

The guardians of Atrato are the national government itself, as well as "ethnic communities living in the Atrato River basin" (Calzadilla 2019, 7; *Tierra Digna*). The court further ordered the formation of a Commission of the Guardians to be subsequently established in order to represent the river. In the Aotearoa New Zealand cases, there was a very careful and innovative parsing through the political motivation for assigning representative powers to certain groups and not others. In the Atrato case, the stereotypical idea of "native" guardianship is particularly stark, as the court identifies local guardians by ethnic criteria, as if being local depended on one's genetic makeup or, conversely, being a miner does. At the same time, the central power of the state cannot be sidestepped, and therefore the very state that was sued because of its gross negligence in defending constitutional rights becomes a guardian! This state, as I argued earlier, already had plenty of laws at its disposal for stopping Amazonian land grabbing or mining with mercury. The court seems to think that it either lacked the appropriate 'consciousness' or else that rights by themselves can do the job the Colombian state has been actively resisting for centuries (because it is part and parcel of its very existence).

Despite the seemingly insufficient order of a bilateral guardianship model for Atrato, local communities seized on the opportunity created by the ruling to develop the model further, for and by themselves. Simply fulfilling the court's order of appointing one guardian from local communities would have been widely insufficient in getting across the multiplicity that is inherent in the river itself and in its human neighbors. As with Whanganui, the river is a being of multiple facets, flowing differently, with different waters in different places, with various speeds and over varied terrain. These kinds of specificities, completely alien to modernist thought, were nonetheless brought in by the local communities themselves when they decided to use the order of the court to create a multiple local guardian made up of 14 different people. These represent the seven local communities interacting with substantively different portions of the river. The communities appointed one male and one female guardian in order to ensure equitable representation. Both moves go beyond the decision of the court itself (Macpherson and Clavijo Ospina 2020, Cagüeñas et al 2020).

Cagüeñas et al (2020) document how communities have invented a forum of dialogue that will slowly parse through the meaning of representing the river. This is also in contrast to the

Māori experience, which already had such representation and was seeking its formal recognition by the state. In the Atrato case, the court order is used for political innovation on the ground, but it is locals themselves that are most aware of the dangers of working together with a state apparatus that has always excluded them. In this case, the local communities do not have any privileged relationship with the Atrato that is recognized by the law, and therefore the new legal person can easily be captured by the state and put to work for an extractivist agenda. This law can be used, for example, to ban *all* artisanal mining, without making the necessary difference between local kinds and mechanized ones. Afterwards, and especially in light of the river's right to restoration, the state can make concessions to mining conglomerates that fill all the necessary permits and promise all the necessary remediation. This, the state can argue, is in the interest of the river and of local people that can be brought out of poverty through organized resource extraction. If this sounds fanciful, it bears mentioning that this is what has happened in Bolivia and, to a lesser extent, in Ecuador (see Chapter 6).

The Colombian Constitutional Court painted a picture of the Atrato River as the victim of greedy "humans", without any identifiable enemies that could in fact be targeted by the law. This kind of judicial proclamation, despite its seemingly strong rhetoric, is therefore very comfortable for the neoliberal state, which can go on scoring minor victories for "environmentalists" while maintaining its de facto course. It propagates stereotypical views of Indigenous and local people and shows its lack of serious commitment to radical solutions in rushing though decisions without any democratic process. The timeline that the court sets for the implementation of its orders is stunning: *four months* for the creation of a medium and long-term plan for the river; five months for an intergenerational agreement.

The contrast with the patient Māori approach is obvious. The culprit for the degradation of Te Urewera is not "humanity", but the colonial state. A correct diagnosis of the ill can therefore lead to innovative solutions. In the Colombian case, the apparatus of policy diffusion that has propagated the idea of guardianship as a totalizing model, while mixing it with particular rights, has influenced the court's judgment decisively.[4] However, local communities have started a necessarily slower process of dialogue that gets closer to the Māori notion of paying attention to a particular place.

Local deliberation has already started to question, for example, the environmental impacts of traditional mining pre-mechanization, and to ask to what extent those can be tolerated. It has also taken an approach that rebukes the claim that locals are ecocentric, inasmuch as they relate to the environment primarily through use. It is very interesting that in this case local communities had not previously been organized as such, nor was there a pre-existing ontological and philosophical system that rendered Atrato in a particular kind of way (Cagüeñas et al 2020). What comes out of this new experiment in river representation can be extremely significant for the future of Atrato, but the court order itself can eventually act as a straitjacket for that kind of innovation, even though it initially spurred it. Instead of the rights of Atrato being the tool that the state lacked for environmental protection, it may prove to be another tool that it can use to exclude locals (so far the state has had very little interest in the local experiments with representation) precisely under the guise of protecting the river.

Ganga and Yamuna

Ganga (also known as the Ganges) is both one of the world's best-known rivers, and one of the most polluted. In 2014, Muhammad Salim, a resident of the riparian town of Hardwar, "initiated public interest litigation in the High Court of Uttarakhand" to ask the court to compel the state to enforce the already existing legal protections of the river (Clark et al 2018, p.813). This case draws on many of the strands already discussed, but also introduces new elements that are significant for the further development of the rights of nature.

4 Coverage of the river rights cases have tended to lump them all together, particularly in media reports. Scholarly works, too, have hastily concluded that Atrato and Whanganui are analogous cases. My argument should cast serious doubts on this assumption.

Initially, the Court ruled in favor of Salim and ordered the State of Uttarakhand to act by forming, within three months, a Ganga Management Board. When this was not respected by the state, the judge – Sharad Sharma – penned another judgment that granted legal personality to Ganga an Yamuna (an important tributary). The High Court ruled that "the Rivers Ganga and Yamuna, all their tributaries, streams, every natural water flowing with flow continuously or intermittently of these rivers, are declared as juristic/legal persons/living entities having the status of a legal person with all corresponding rights, duties and liabilities, of a living person in order to preserve and conserve river Ganga and Yamuna" (UHC 2017, 11). The Court also ordered three specific government agencies to act as guardians of the river, explicitly using the doctrine of *in loco parentis*, the same doctrine used to appoint guardians to children or incapacitated adult humans. In this judgment the doctrine is explicit, whereas in other guardianship models it is merely implicit.

As part of the motivation for this decision the Court argued that the two rivers are "worshipped by Hindus. These rivers are very sacred and revered. […] Thus, to protect the recognition and the faith of society, Rivers Ganga and Yamuna are required to be declared as the legal persons/living persons" (IHC 2017, 4, 11). Immediately after this judgment, the appointed guardians appealed to the Supreme Court, which swiftly stayed the original order. The case is yet to be decided. Regardless of the eventual outcome, it is a very useful one to illustrate the complex interplay of totality thinking with local specificities.

The fact that the rights of nature are travelling to diverse places has been understood as a process of international policy diffusion, most notably by Kauffman and Martin (2017b). As we have seen, it makes sense to see these cases as being inspired by other instances elsewhere, most notably Ecuador, Bolivia, and New Zealand, which have become paradigmatic in their own ways. As scholarship has shown, the most instrumental organizations in diffusing rights for nature laws have been the Global Alliance for the Rights of Nature

(GARN), CELDF[5] (already encountered earlier), and the UN Harmony with Nature Knowledge Network. These organizations have also become important in proposing rights for nature at the international legal level. The mechanism of policy diffusion pass, as Kauffman and Martin point out, through these channels.

Equally important has been the international press coverage of rights of nature cases, starting with Ecuador and really coming into its own with New Zealand. Whereas Ecuador could have seemed like an outlier, the New Zealand developments, and their assimilation by international media into fundamentally the same kind of case, has given a lot of hope that we are witnessing a growing trend that will increasingly influence laws in many different places. These mediatic channels are themselves influenced by the international policy network as to the general framework in which rights of nature are presented. These cases offer easy pickings for hopeful media coverage in a world awash in environmental doom. But they are also routinely inaccurate and very scant on details. For example, the very separate histories of Ecuador and New Zealand are almost always lumped together. This is also the case in coverage of the Indian judgment. Scholarship has been much more careful, of course, but also there, it is commonplace to see the Whanganui case presented as one of guardianship, and to see most cases of rights presented as 'emanating' from indigenous worldviews (with some exceptions of Macpherson, O'Donnell, and Sanders).

The case of Ganga and Yamuna, like that of Atrato, is influenced by the false presentation of Whanganui as a case of guardianship. Whereas in Ecuador, as we have seen, the issue of guardianship was not addressed, the New Zealand cases have generally been understood as only offering this innovation to theory and practice. The careful way in which Māori legal tradition has in fact subverted the ideas of rights and guardianship has been mostly unremarked. This subversion is itself good proof of the uneasy conceptual relationship

5 Recently, the original founders of CELDF have started another organization, the Center for Democratic and Environmental Rights (CDER). As apparent from the title itself, the issue of rights became even more entrenched than before.

between rights and indigenous thinking, but the rights of nature have continued to be presented as coming out of, or 'translating', indigenous conceptions. The alliance between rights and national states has also been sidelined (with the notable exception of Rawson and Mansfield 2018).

The way in which the ecotheological history of rights has managed to become dominant and largely unquestioned matters because policy diffusion tends to happen along lines steeped in totality and with a moralistic framing of environmental harm. In the Indian case, moralizing nature came under the guise of the religious significance of the river, which is revered by many in India, though the Court only recognized its significance to Hindus. The plaintiff himself did not present his case in terms of religious significance; it was the judge that took the opportunity to introduce the idea that the religious/moral personality of the river deserves legal recognition.

In the Indian context, the idea of a juristic persons has a long history, going back to British colonial rule (Alley 2019, Berti 2021, Patel 2010). In the mid 19th century, the British introduced this concept so they could handle the complexities surrounding religious idols. They therefore used juristic person to format the being of idols in law. They were particularly interested in being able "to decide land, property, and entitlement disputes" (Alley 2019, p.4). As Doctor (2018) further explains, the juridical personhood of a religious idol "avoided having to sift through all the claims of tradition, while also neatly appearing to respect Indian sentiments by treating the idols as living persons" (in Alley, idem). The practice of legally personifying religious idols survived British rule and became a commonplace way of handling disputes over ownership, particularly in cases that involved gifts and other kinds of property being given to an idol by worshipers through, for example, wills.

The idea of juristic person grants idols the ownership of assets. This means that the goods of the idol are not public goods, but neither are they fully private, because they are supposed to be used for funding rituals and supporting pilgrimage (Alley 2019, Das Acevedo 2018). One of the key motivations of the Indian judiciary in upholding legal personhood of this kind has also been to facilitate the paying of taxes by idols, which can file their income declarations through their guardians, which are to take care of the idol as they would of an infant. The ownership of temple assets by the personified deity has given rise to different kinds of judicial decisions, adjudicating which deity can own which assets, how many deities can be owners, and so on (Berti 2021). This is to say that the interpretation of legal personhood for idols is a matter of continuous dispute, though the mechanism itself is widely accepted.

In recognizing the personhood of deities, judges do not necessarily attach it to a particular image, or embodiment, of the idol (in an object or statue). What is recognized are the human *purposes* embedded in such images, and in this sense idol personality is a recognition of human interests that are expressed through religious form. Colas (2012) argues that religious scholars are not unproblematically enthusiastic about the idea that idols are persons that can own assets. Idol personality "is hypothetical and has to be taken as a socio-religious convention" (in Berti 2021). Idol jurisprudence looks like idol politics because it ultimately adjudicates, as it was originally intended to do, between different ways of employing wealth that empower certain groups over others. Through this differential apportionment, different rituals or pilgrimages are promoted; different conceptions of right conduct, or rights to access religious sites, are weighted against each other.

For example, a controversial 1991 state-level decision, reversed by the Supreme Court, ruled that God Ayyappan, of the Sabarimala temple, did not wish to allow women between the ages of 10 and 50 (so of menstruating age; see Alley 2019) to enter the premises. The Kerala Hight Court justified its judgment by arguing that the deity "was conceived in the form of a renunciant" and he therefore expressed "the wish to continue to live in celibacy and austerity without being disturbed by the presence of women" (Berti 2021). Ayyappan evidently channeled sexist beliefs, but as lord of his assets he in principle had a right to them – an idea clearly justified by the High Court. I have pointed out consistently how rights of nature can be used selectively to bolster already existing power relations. This seems to also be the case for idol personality.

In the Indian legal tradition, there is a long history of public interest litigation. Unlike in the US, everyone can have standing to sue if done in the name of a public interest, which means that the kind of theory that Cristopher Stone proposed has less purchase in this context. In fact, this doctrine has given rise to judicial activism, because it allows "judges to use suo motu powers to bring a case forward without a petitioner" (Alley 2019, p.6), meaning that they can initiate action of their own accord. This is partly what happened in the Ganga and Yamuna case, where the plaintiff did not ask for legal recognition of the kind granted.

The reasons why the judge decided to grant legal personhood to Ganga and Yamuna are to some extent opaque, but it can be said that the international diffusion of the rights of nature had an important role to play, while interacting with a local legal tradition that inflected the case in specific ways. Given that Ganga is also a deity in Hindu religious traditions – Mother Goddess[6] – Judge Sharma used the idea of juristic person for deities to frame the river as just such a deity. This parallel is not explicit in the judgment but given the Indian legal context it is obvious that it informed the underlying thinking. The rights of the sacred rivers also departed from this tradition in important ways. The river, by becoming a legal person, does not also become self-owning, as in the case of Te Urewera. It does not have property, like other idols do. Instead, its personality is purely fictitious and attached to religious custom in loose ways so that it could introduce the idea of guardianship, which is where the legal proclamation connects with practice.

Judge Sharma charged the director of the national program Clean Ganga, the chief secretary of Uttarakhand, and the advocate general of the state, to be river guardians. The *parens patriae* doctrine is the basis for guardianship, the same doctrine used for minors and people that otherwise cannot fulfill, for different reasons, their own rights and obligations. Unlike in the New Zealand and Colombian cases, this is a more paternalistic view of rivers that are in the same breath pronounced to be sacred and to have the same rights as humans. In interviews with Varanasi residents,[7] Kelly Alley discovered that many did not share the idea that Ganga

6 It is important to note that the gendering is of the river, not of nature as such.

7 Varanasi is on the Ganges, but is not in the state of Uttarakhand.

is a person – she is a God, nor that people could take care of her as parents, seeing that *she* is the Mother. This refusal to think in the same terms as the legal pronouncement reveals the distance between the decidedly top-down, elite judgment and the ways in which people that have relationships with the river conceptualize its existence.

The misalignment between the Court judgment and that of Varanasi residents has several levels. First and perhaps foremost, residents deeply distrust the state, for good reason. Central and regional bureaucracies have not lived up to official promises in terms of pollution reduction and the restoration of the river's health. Therefore, the appointment of state officials as guardians seems, at best, suspect. Secondly, religious framings around Ganga as goddess stress its independence from humans, as well as its own life that will, at some point, end. Alley reports one resident as saying that "thousands of years from now Ganga will not be here. After thousands of years, she will be gone. There will be rivers but not Ganga. Like the Saraswati river in Allahabad is finished. Yamuna river will also go like this" (p.10).

Grounded ways of thinking about the river, and most importantly of understanding human – river – deity relationships, escape the simple pronouncements of the law. In this sense, the concept of juristic person is in line with its British beginnings, as a mechanism of cutting through complexities. Ganga will die, and others will take her place, as the manifestations of deities are mutable. She cannot be vulnerable, or in need of protection, because she is all powerful. The way in which these conceptions relate to efforts at pollution reduction, for example, is a question to be asked, and a very important one. But it cannot be answered through simply declaring the river to be a legal person, precisely because this formulation was neither initiated by communities, nor does it seem to be widely accepted by them. It does not 'translate' their way of thinking.

Perhaps most surprisingly, the Court's decision on guardianship was not accepted by the guardians themselves. They promptly appealed to the authority of the Supreme court, which stayed the lower Court's decision. A guardian as construed by the Court would be fully responsible for the actions of the river, something explicitly stated in the judgment. The Supreme Court wondered if flood victims could then sue the state – the parent of the river, really – for damages. It also justified its decision by noting that Ganga flows through several states, and it is unclear whether the judgment issued in Uttarakhand would apply to downstream states, and whether the parents of the minor would be responsible for pollution initiated in their state that would inevitably cross administrative borders.

The Court of Uttarakhand also used the mechanism of legal personality for mountains and glaciers. As the court states in the glaciers case, "a juristic person can be any subject matter other than a human being to which the law attributes personality for good and sufficient reasons" (Glaciers, 62-3). But, as O'Donnell (2018) shows, the doctrine of legal personality is extended to its maximum girth in being conflated with the notions of living entity, as well as "legal entity/legal person/juristic person/juridical person/moral person/artificial person" (138). Many of these concepts invoked by the Court are synonyms of the juridical person idea established in Indian legal tradition. But the inclusion of moral person/artificial person raises questions, not least about the relationship between moral and legal personality in a deeply religiously inflected context, as well as the meaning of artificiality side-by-side with supposedly obvious moral values. This seems to elevate potentially anything to the status of legal person as an ontological category, therefore emptying the power of the ontological by relegating it to whim.

The Indian case is good at showing further dendrites connecting the state and the rights of nature. The court identified the rivers Ganga and Yamuna as being sacred to Hindus, omitting to say anything about its status to other groups. Given Hindu nationalism and its influence on the Indian state, this may be dangerous (O'Donnell 2018). Vrinda Narain argues that "in the context of rising Hindu right-wing rhetoric, the Court's linking of the Hindu faith with national identity and the corresponding casting out of religious minorities implied by this method of argumentation by the court is cause for concern" (in Clark et al 2018, p.816). The potential nationalist uses of Ganga's legal personality have so far not materialized. Instead, the nationalist government that holds power both at state and central levels has distanced itself from the ruling, as evidence by their appealing to the Supreme Court.

If the Supreme Court judgment upholds the legal personality of the rivers, the avenue towards nationalism may as well be exploited. This can be done in two ways. First, the original judgment mandates participation of local communities. This kind of top-down mandate for participation rings hollow, as true participation tends to travel the other way around. Be that as it may, it is not a stretch to imagine that whatever participation may come about would be restricted to Hindus, because Ganga and Yamuna are *their* idols. Second, the Court adopted a very wide definition of environmental harm, stating that even the "plucking of one leaf" constitutes harm. Given current levels of pollution (also tied to industries promoted by the state), this is an extreme interpretation of what the law may achieve and of what may constitute harm. It seems to be a radical application of ecocentrism that may be combined with Hindu nationalism in potentially discriminatory ways. Is every person's plucking equal? Whatever may happen in the future of this judgment, it is safe to say that it gives more tools to the state than it takes away, regardless of the intentions motivating it.

The kind of ecocentrism that rights of nature have inherited is steeped in ecotheology. The Indian cases show this to be true from the perspective of polytheistic religions as well. Alley (2019) calls the framework at work here "spiritual ecology" (or sacred ecology). Spiritually inflected ecology is very old and common (see Berkes 2017), and on account of that also very varied. The Court ruling, however, is not based in the specificity of sacred *ecological* practices, but rather uses religious/legal personality to gloss over the existing relationships that construe the river (along its 2500km!) in different ways. This seems to be a different kind of ecotheology, not a sacred ecology.

As with all cases of rights of nature, close attention needs to be paid to the local contexts in which they appear. The Indian local traditions, in religious, political, and legal senses, have had a decisive influence on this case, but they also combined with the idea of the rights of nature being fundamentally ecocentric and applicable everywhere in more or less the same ways. Though it may seem that this case is tailored to particular needs – the pollution of the river, as well as particular beliefs – the holiness of the river, it trades much more in modernist abstractions cemented into legal traditions borrowed from Europeans. In fact, there is no local participation to speak of.

As high-minded as the Court may have been, it could not help but sneak into its pronouncement problems that can only be solved by going into the specific relationships that people entertain, as well as through tailored mechanisms of enforcement. The Court did not develop any kind of institutional or participatory framework to see through the protection of the rivers. It simply mandated guardians, who do not want to act as such. It gave the juristic person no funds, and no property. It said nothing about already existing interests in the river. And it is unclear how it interacts with already existing laws, which already prohibit much of what the Court wanted to prohibit.

This case renders the mechanism of judicial pronouncement for achieving rights of nature suspect, and should raise doubts regarding the dominant mechanisms of policy diffusion and on what they accomplish. The assumption that rights are primarily about ecocentric values and the protection of nature (as opposed to being primarily about new political configurations that may play in the favor of the state) has incentivized their presentation as all part of the same movement, a claim I will investigate in the next chapter. This has meant that any law, however contextually different or problematic, is quickly adopted as proof that the movement is gaining steam and that the world is finally turning towards ecocentric law. This has been further bolstered by the promotion of rights of nature as an international level solution, a strategy to which I now turn.

Universal Declarations

The history of human rights would not be the same without its Universal Declaration, a document that internationalized human rights while also laying an international framework for their protection. Similarly, rights of nature advocates have looked towards the international arena since before the case of Ecuador. In fact, the case of

Ecuador itself was partly motivated by the ambition to gain international prominence, as I have documented in Tănăsescu (2013, 2016). This is why the first attempt to apply the Ecuadorian provisions was by using the idea that these constitutional rights apply extraterritorially (like human rights do). A group of plaintiffs, most involved with the drafting of Ecuador's constitution, sued BP for the Gulf of Mexico Deepwater Horizon oil leak on the grounds that it violated the rights of nature enshrined in the Ecuadorian constitution. The lawsuit went nowhere, but the point was not to actually win; the point was to make an international entry and to popularize the idea that rights of nature can, and should, become international law.

Several years later, in 2010, and with the explicit support of Evo Morales, then Bolivia's president, a Universal Declaration for the Rights of Mother Earth[8] was drafted and presented to the UN for consideration. Advocates modelled it explicitly on human rights declarations of the 20th century, believing that its adoption will usher in a new, international era of rights of nature. This may be so; and it may also be that the more cases at all legal levels there are, the more this kind of universal declaration stands a chance of being adopted. What is interesting from a critical perspective is to assess the intellectual genealogy of this proposal as well its relationship with liberal rights discourse.

It would be repetitive to dwell too much on the expression Mother Earth, as I have already pointed out the problematic gendering of nature that it accomplishes. The Universal Declaration for the Rights of Mother Earth would impose this kind of gendering everywhere through its adoption at the UN level. This, to my mind, would be a blow to indigenous conceptions, which are much more multidimensional and variegated. This kind of gendering accord well with ecotheology. And as Tola (2018) points out, it also goes seamlessly with the neoliberal idea that nature is first and foremost a producer, just like the stereotypical image of motherhood as fertility would suggest.

It may, however, be instructive to pause on how some indigenous philosophical traditions conceptualize the environment in

---

8 Available here: https://www.therightsofnature.org/universal-declaration/

non-gendered ways. Merata Kawharu, writing specifically about Māori relations with the environment, explains that the surrounding world is conceptualized (and lived) as a living ancestor. This conception is given succinct expression in the saying "Māori walk backwards into the future" (p.222), which means that present generations take their cues from stories about past deeds of important ancestors. These past actions are mostly in relation to specific environments, which are in some sense personified, but in ways that need not be explicit about gender. Creation myths, too, portray the world as both male and female (Ranginui and Papatuánuku). The productivity of nature, which leads western conceptions towards the idea of Mother, is recognized through gender relations, or else through ancestor – environment relations. The gender of the ancestor is irrelevant, as the accent falls on her/his deeds.

If the environment is to be likened to anything, in Kawharu's account, it is not a person, nor a particular gender. Instead, it is akin to a *marae*, "forums where tikanga or customs are performed, discussed, and negotiated" (p.221). Notice that this is a dynamic, processual rendering of customary law itself, which is amenable to discussion and negotiation, as it is within any living culture. "The meeting house" (the physical one, *whare whakairo*), Pakariki Harrison explains, "is conceptualized metaphorically as a human body, usually representing the eponymous ancestor of a tribe" (in Kawharu 2010, p.228). He goes on to explain how the different parts of the building, elaborated in the famous Māori wood-carving style, represent parts of a body, such that inside the building people are held within the ancestor, just like they are held within the surrounding environment. The gender of the ancestor is not transferred to the environment. If we though that way, nature here would be male, given that tribal leaders were mostly men.

The environment as *marae* therefore consists of two different concepts: the body of the living ancestor, symbolized in the physical building, and the correct (or incorrect, as the case may be) way of acting that is informed by the relationship between ancestors and places. James Henare expresses the relationship between these two concepts thus: "when I look at these landscapes I see my ancestors walking back to me" (in Kawharu, p.228).

In contrast to these textured conceptions, totality thinking is most starkly expressed in the Universal Declaration. It is framed to emanate from "we, the people and nations of Earth", which may very well be interpreted as a synonym for "humanity". The text of the declaration also makes the claim that human rights cannot exist without nature's rights because humans are part of nature. This claim accomplishes two things: it clearly establishes the genealogical connection between liberal human rights and rights of nature without engaging with the problems that it may pose; and it hides the many ways in which human rights and nature's rights are at odds, as we have already seen in the analysis of cases.

The language of the declaration also raises other fundamental questions. For example, it speaks of Mother Earth as both a living and indivisible being, while also granting rights (at the very least the right to exist) to all specific beings. Presumably, this includes all known pathogens as well as charismatic animals. In fact, it may include more, as the declaration also extends its protection to the abiotic realm, in an apparent nod to indigenous thinking. In practice, a declaration worded through an unreflective repetition of ecotheology would mean that powerful actors, including first and foremost states and multinational corporations, could use it selectively, as has so far happened in Ecuador and Bolivia (see Chapter 6). As has been firmly established, this would be largely to the detriment of the already disenfranchised.

Traces of the perpetuation of disenfranchisement through rights are already visible in certain key omission from the Universal Declaration as well as in the Colombian Atrato case. In the former, the only perceived enemy of nature is "capitalism", which has the benefit of at least getting closer to identifying a culprit but remains completely silent as to the crucial role of nation states in silencing revolt against the dominant mode of political economy. In the Atrato case, the court ruling was occasioned by illegal mining, but the court identifies as the ultimate culprit the human species, omitting to mention that illegal miners are often poor and excluded populations that are forced into that way of life by government policy. Rights of nature ire against illegal miners has also been expressed in Ecuador during one of the first cases of constitutional protection for nature's rights in the country. In that case, the Ecuadorian state used nature's rights to evict small-scale artisanal miners in a remote region of the country (Daly 2012). The same state that evicted artisanal miners has, since 2008, expanded corporate mining, often in indigenous territories.

Rights liberalism has evolved to be a growing kaleidoscope of rights that are incompatible with each other and therefore remain at the mercy of the state for resolution and effective application. This point has been made by many critical scholars of human rights (see for example Douzinas 2000), who show that the supposedly universal rights of humans are always differentially applied to suit the agenda of the nation state. Migrants don't have the same rights as citizens, for example. Human rights are inseparable from citizenship rights, which are their channel towards effective protection. In particular, socio-economic status has a decisive impact on one's human rights, as the poor are routinely treated as rightless and subjected to paternalistic state surveillance.

Similarly, the rights of nature add to the liberal kaleidoscope a tool for the state to satisfy certain environmental interests while advancing its largely extractivist agenda. Under conditions of a globalized capitalist economy, this will continue even if the world transitions to renewable energy, which is itself extractive of land and many other resources used in its production. As Bruno Latour pointed out in a public lecture delivered in 2021, the goal of mainstream political economy seems to be to pursue a kind of Total Production, where everything is integrated within a productive apparatus that yields 'economic value', whether in the form of 'ecosystem services' or consumer goods. Surely despite the best intentions of advocates, ecotheological rights participate in this dream of Total Production by extending rights to everything, while undermining radically different forms of living in particular places, as championed by many Indigenous Populations.

The rights of nature do not *inherently* do this. I have argued that a certain *kind* of rights, enamored with totality and completely uncritical of its own intellectual inheritance, can – perhaps despite themselves – do this. But the rights of nature harbor other possibilities as well, and the New Zealand cases are instructive here. If nothing else, advocates should be thanked for ushering in a new era of legal innovation. But like so much other legal and political innovation, the settling of orthodoxy risks uprooting the initial radical potential of the new idea. Hence critique is crucial, in order to be lucid about unintended consequences and to keep the innovative impetus alive.

In the next chapter, I will examine how the critique offered so far can help move the rights of nature towards a greater diversity of practice. I will also look at how practical experimentation and diversification can change our theoretical models for the better. Finally, we will see what legal innovation outside the hegemony of totality may look like and how rights advocacy can participate by becoming conscious of the inherently political nature of their favorite tool.

Chapter VI: From Practice to Theory

The many different cases presented so far show a diversifying toolbox that is used for multiple purposes. But how can the diversity of practice be reflected in diversity of theory, and how can it in turn inform future cases? A process of reflective learning is crucial in order to both avoid the settling in of orthodoxy and keep advocacy open towards yet unknown possibilities.

To draw out the various insights useful for further development in both theory and practice, I want to look at some court cases that already show, in practice, some of the theoretical tensions I have pointed out. In particular, these clarify the essential role of the state in rights of nature. After doing this, I will discuss a series of crucial ideas for the rights of nature that need to be rethought. I will start with looking one last time at the relationship between indigeneity and rights so as to open up new avenues for Indigenous empowerment that look beyond the concept of right. I will re-examine the idea of legal person with a particular focus on the *person* as a model for what counts (legally, politically, ethically). Indigenous thought offers plenty of resources for decentering the person in legal and political thought.

The last sections think about what a critical engagement with rights suggests for further practice. I argue that the crucial question is not what rights nature may have, but rather who is entitled to speak for nature. In other words, the role of political representation is central in all rights of nature practice and should be better reflected in theory. Lastly, I will examine whether the rights of nature can, at this point in their history, count as a movement. The claim that all cases so far are part of a movement is so ubiquitous as to need no particular reference. The expression "the movement for rights of nature" has become a habit for advocates and commentators. I will examine in detail whether this claim is warranted, and I will argue that it risks hiding the diversity of practice in favor of ecotheological orthodoxy. In order to restore diversity, we need to think much more critically about what makes a movement, and how movements themselves need to remain open to unpredictable possibilities.

Some Court Cases

Most rights of nature laws so far have been untested in court. The discussion developed in this book should help anticipate the diversity of cases that will ensue in the next decades, with results ranging widely. The expected, and so far witnessed, variation in results follows from the conceptual and practical diversity of rights for nature as well as from the different contexts in which they have appeared. The purposes motivating different legal provisions vary, and therefore their application will as well. Even if there haven't yet been a lot of legal cases to speak of, some of the earliest installments of rights of nature have been tested in court. This is the case in Ecuador, where there are already several court cases that can be examined. And they already show the practical consequences of many of the theoretical ambiguities explored.

The most widely covered case so far is also the first one in the country, namely the protection of the rights of Vilcabamba river. The plaintiffs sued the municipal government for having modified the course of the river through a road construction project. The municipal government undertook the expansion project without having the necessary environmental impact assessments. The resultant material from the construction project was dumped in the river, and this caused a modification of its course, which then resulted in flooding the downstream property of riparian landowners. These sued the municipal government using the constitutional rights of nature provisions adopted in 2008.

The landowners could have also sued for damage to their property, but they did not, instead choosing the mechanism of nature's rights. As I have argued in Tănăsescu (2016), the wide standing that the constitution grants for the legal representation of nature is shown to also have a connection with the issue of property. Though advocates routinely claim that the rights of nature are opposed to property rights, this is not necessarily so. The Loja provincial court recognized the legal standing of the riparian owners also because they were directly interested in the fate of their property, now partly flooded. This makes perfect sense, and other legislation (for example, the New Zealand cases) already takes into account the special relationship that obtains between places and their owners.

The local government was ordered to remedy the harm caused to the river and issue a public apology. The remediation has been quite slow to materialize. In principle, the river is supposed to be turned back to the state that the riparian owners preferred. However, if restoration is to be understood strictly, then the rights of nature could also have been used against riparian owners, for the return of the river to some earlier state. However that may be, the potential tension between human and nature's rights was resolved by the judge apparently in favor of nature. He explicitly stated that the right to a healthy environment is more important than the right to a better road, even though this is weighing two different kinds of *human* rights against each other. In this case, the judge imposed this particular hierarchy of rights, but there is nothing definitive in the Ecuadorian constitution that obliges judges to reach the same decision elsewhere. The constitution in fact states that all of its many rights are on the same level of importance. This is impossible to implement in practice, where decisions will have to prioritize some rights over others, thus leaving ample room for interpretation. Human rights jurisprudence especially has as a core task the balancing of rights.

This wide interpretive space is even better exemplified in another case in Ecuador, namely the Mirador case of 2013. Here, an alliance of Indigenous Groups and environmental NGOs sued a mining conglomerate and the state for violation of nature's rights in a planned mining operation in the Cordillera del Cóndor, a hyper biodiverse region of the country and also home to Indigenous populations. The plaintiffs sued because the mining concession was approved by the relevant ministries, and they alleged that this concession would violate several rights given by the constitution, including the rights of nature. They also claimed that the precautionary principle enshrined in the constitution would be violated by the planned mining activities.

Unlike in the Vilcabamba case (which, it is important to keep in mind, was a small-scale project of little national importance), the company planning to do the mining – Ecuacorriente S.A. – had undertaken all necessary environmental impact studies, which were approved by the resource and environmental ministries. The judge ruled that, because all of the necessary documentation had been correctly filled, there was no basis for the plaintiffs to assume rights were being violated. Furthermore, the alleged violation was supposed to happen in the future, and therefore the plaintiffs had no basis to claim that it would in fact happen.

The judge interpreted the *buen vivir* doctrine enshrined in the Ecuadorian constitution as requiring a level of resource extraction and argued that there is no inherent reason why such extraction cannot be done in an environmentally responsible manner. Here, the weighing of nature's rights against the human right to development was done in favor of the latter, clearly understood as the prerogative of a modern state that needs to be integrated within a global economic system predicated on consumptive lifestyles. Although this decision was obviously unpopular with rights of nature advocates, it is no faultier than the Vilcabamba one. Both of them operate within the wide margin of interpretation that the constitution makes possible. Considering these cases together, it becomes clear just how important the political dimension of the rights of nature is. In fact, we can only understand such cases by thinking about them as instances of political weighing of interests that, in any particular case, may run in incompatible directions.

To this end, the important role played by the environmental assessment documents is telling. In the Vilcabamba case, it was their absence that occasioned the lawsuit and figured greatly in the decision of the court. In the Mirador case, their existence – in fact, the defendant's compliance with the law – also proved crucial, but in the opposite direction. CELDF, the American organization instrumental in codifying the Ecuadorian constitutional provisions, has long argued that granting rights to nature would overcome the role of the state as mere regulator of environmental harm. In their view, things like environmental impact assessments simply tell companies how they can be allowed to do damage. The rights of nature, they argue, would be a solution to this problem. In practice, however, these kinds of impact assessments prove to be very sticky indeed. In the context of already existing rights of nature, judges will still have to decide whether the defendants have complied with existing law (which requires impact assessments). If they have, it will still be very hard to forbid resource extraction, especially because the neoliberal state committed to it, nature's rights notwithstanding. As I argued previously, the state is comfortable with rights and knows how to bend them as it suits political and economic elites.

Though this particular case doesn't immediately show the problems raised by nature's right to restoration, it does open up a speculative space where these problems can be explored. In philosophical debates on the meaning of restoration, one of the greatest issues identified by philosophers (see Elliot 2008, Katz 2009, 2012) has been the problem of "moral hazard". Restoration started its life as a technical solution to industrial disruption of environmental conditions. It really took off in the late 20th century, when the belief that humans can turn environments back really took hold, largely because of advances in restoration techniques. However, the idea that one can return a place to a previous state in a sense incentivizes extractivism, because it is now possible – at least on paper – to extract while only temporarily disrupting. This is the issue of moral hazard, namely that restoration can act as an incentive, as just another box to tick in order to be allowed to progress with the project of modern development.

While the idea of moral hazard is not the only way of assessing restoration, it is a real problem in baseline-specific projects. Where the target of restoration is a particular past *composition* of the environment (known as a baseline), it is easy to see how extractive industries can promise to turn back the clock. This, in fact, already routinely happens, and whether such promises are kept or not is then subject to lengthy litigation.[1] Additionally, only large industry players can even promise to restore, precisely because of the costs involved and the technical expertise required. Thus, enshrining a right to restoration without specifying what this means immediately opens the possibility of empowering extractive industries. This is implicit in the Mirador case, in which the judge obviously thought that mining can be done in a responsible manner, which includes the remediation of a site after extraction is complete. In future cases, this use of restoration may as well become explicit.

The role of the state is clear in the Mirador case, particularly because the sentence was specifically justified in terms of the duty of the State to "develop" and, in so doing, to protect the liberal rights of its citizens (some of whom count more than others). The inherent tensions in the liberal rights concept and its constructive relation with modern nation states can be contemplated here in its practical effect. These effects are also in line with the political moment. Rafael Correa, president of Ecuador at the time of this case, made clear his position that development is paramount and that it can be pursued whilst respecting the environment. Extractive industries under the Correa government expanded at an unprecedented rate (Lalander 2014), and they were explicitly justified through both nationalism (the nation state, not corporations, must reap the benefits) and progressive policies of redistribution (funding healthcare, education, infrastructure for the poor).

This, what Gudynas (2009) has called progressive neo-extractivism, functions very well with a panoply of rights that it selectively activates. In this selective activation, several things help greatly. On the one hand, the vague standing requirements of the Ecuadorian constitution are incredibly helpful. On the other, the gendering of nature, as I have argued previously with support from the work of Tola (2018), works in favor of extractivism.

The first point is best seen in the use of rights for nature by the Ecuadorian state itself to clear the way for large-scale mining. The state, this time as plaintiff, sued artisanal miners and argued that

1 See the famous Chevron-Texaco case in Ecuador.

"'the illegal mining was polluting the Santiago, Bogotá, Ónzole and Cayapas rivers, thereby violating the rights of nature. Two months later, the Second Court of Criminal Guarantees of Pichincha issued the injunction 'for the protection of the rights of nature and of the people'" (Daly, 2012). Subsequently, army personnel cleared the area of artisanal miners (largely impoverished populations forced into precarious labor) and confiscated or destroyed their property. At the same time, the national government expanded its mining concessions to both state and multinational actors. This kind of use of the rights of nature may seem like a perversion to advocates, but it is not: It is well within the logic of what the Ecuadorian constitution provided bases for.

The second point – the problematic gendering of nature as Mother Earth – is better seen by switching to Bolivia. There this gendering has been explicitly used in relation to resource generation (and, logically, extraction). Generation is the counterpart of the nurturing aspect of femininity stereotypically applied to motherhood. Rights of nature advocates routinely use this portrayal as if it were an unproblematic fact. In Bolivia, as in Ecuador, the government of Evo Morales has expanded natural resource exploitation with largely similar justifications (development and progressive redistribution of the supposed benefits). And it has specifically used the image of Mother Earth in order to achieve this.

Morales, for example, has inaugurated the first Chinese pilot plant for producing lithium-ion batteries, an increasingly crucial part of the global drive towards "green growth". These batteries are fundamental for, among other gadgets, electric vehicles, which governments the world over are promoting at increasing rates. Morales framed the lithium reserves of Bolivia as a generous gift of Mother Earth, part and parcel of its nurturing its people. Lalander (2014, 169) quotes him as saying that "Bolivia has the largest lithium reserves of the entire world, that's our Mother Earth. [...] You could not imagine how Mother Nature provides us natural resources". Wouldn't it be foolish, the implication goes, to leave those underground? Wouldn't it be a betrayal of the gifts of nature, that could be used for socially progressive purposes? It is easy to be outraged at this kind of rhetoric, but it is in fact already sanctioned by the conceptual apparatus explored throughout this book.

There are several other Ecuadorian court cases currently ongoing. So far, of the 13 Ecuadorian cases that have reached final decisions and that Kauffman and Martin (2017a) document, none of those brought by the government were lost. It remains to be seen whether this kind of state bias continues, but the kinds of issues brought out at the intersection of theory and practice are there to stay (at least until the law changes), and they offer great learning possibilities for what is an experimental and evolving practice.

One could expect similar patterns to emerge in future cases where ecotheological rights for nature have been enshrined. The wide variation in outcome between the various extant court cases[2] reveals the problems inherent in a formulation of nature's rights based on a universal subject (nature as person) and wide standing. It remains an open question how other cases, from New Zealand to Colombia, as well as future ones, will play out in practice. For now, there isn't enough empirical evidence to decide, but based on the theory explored I would expect, particularly in the New Zealand cases, further empowerment of Māori groups as well as selective resource development, which does not inherently contradict Māori views. The kind of implementation explored in Ecuador and Bolivia is very difficult to pull off under the New Zealand conditions, which all but preclude it. This is itself an important lesson: paying attention to detailed representative arrangements is very important for what nature's rights may end up doing.

Indigeneity and Personhood

Though Indigenous People started out as allies of the Ecuadorian and Bolivian governments, they soon fell out. This is a continuation of the always antagonistic relationship between Indigenous communities and the nation state. Ever since the earliest history of colonization, Indigenous People have had to adapt to the increasingly

2 Also see Tănăsescu (2016, 129-132).

powerful presence of the state while keeping alive traditions and ways of knowing and thinking that are radically different from the premises of nationalism. Even though the rights of nature initially appeared to bolster indigenous rights, the very concept of rights itself should have alerted advocates to more ambiguous results. Indeed, Indigenous communities in Ecuador and Bolivia have been confronted by yet another case of the state selectively using rights to further its agenda, often at their expense.

The supposedly inherent relationship between the rights of nature and indigeneity has become a trope of scholarship and news coverage. These rights are often presented as emanating from, or translating, indigenous thinking. I have already argued against this view (also see Tănăsescu 2020) extensively.[3] Here, I want to complement that argument with one last element which is revealed by the variation in practical applications of rights for nature laws. The legal person status of nature is very often seen as the bridge between indigenous and western legal conceptions. In the case of Mother Earth, for example, the case for its supposed personality has been forcefully made, and also forcefully tied to indigeneity. However, the way in which indigenous thinking conceptualizes the environment is much more diverse than that and, as I will argue, is not particularly helped by the notions of person or personality.

Critical legal scholarship has started to uncover the moral roots of the concept of legal *person* as well as the tautological relationship it has with the concept of rights. Costas Douzinas, for example, argues that "for the liberal philosophy of personhood, human rights belong to 'normal' people" (in Gearty and Douzinas 2012, 65). He goes on to show that normality is itself constructed in such a way as to exclude undesirable people. Joanna Bourke (2011), in *What It Means to be Human*, shows this in detail, demonstrating how ideas of normal personhood have been used throughout the history of liberalism to exclude women, immigrants, and racialized minorities.

3 But see O'Donnell et al (2020) for a nuanced view of Indigenous involvement in the rights of nature. Despite the nuance, I think most of my critique still holds.

Douzinas further shows that this kind of exclusion is not an aberration of rights theory, but the logical application of its tautological identification of rights with a particular kind of person. Today, it is undeniable that "immigrants, refugees and the poor" are not part of the rights paradigm, even as this paradigm has become the only ideology available in our otherwise post-everything world.

Naffine (2003, 2011), Grear (2013), and Davies (2012) lend further support to the view that the idea of legal personality and its automatic implication in rights theory and practice, derives from a standard imposed by the "normal human individual". Arstein-Kerslake (2017) has shown how the model legal person has routinely excluded people with disabilities or with identities that differ from the moral standard inherent in the concept. What I also want to point out is that the idea of conformity to a standard, in the history of liberalism, understands the person as an *individual*. The rights of the legal person are therefore primarily the rights of an individual qua individual.

It is in the individuality of the person that liberalism finds the foundation for its rights claims. It is the individual that is inviolable, that has rights, and that lends its atomic separation from everything else to the notion of the person. In Western philosophy, the prototypical liberal subject is the Cartesian individual, separated from everything else and alone with his thoughts, through which he comes to know his need and desires. "This conception of personhood becomes the basis for methodological and moral individualism: society exists for the promotion of individual purposes" (Gearty and Douzinas 2012, 71).

Though it is harder and harder to state this today, rights are fictions just as the idea of legal personality is one. To paraphrase Douzinas, there is no right to rights. In other words, rights are not discovered, but invented, proclaimed, given. To make this argument is not to say that rights have no function, or no basis whatsoever, but it is to say that they are not the panacea they claim to be simply because they are grounded in the individual human body.

As Samuel Moyn argues, in *The Last Utopia* (2012), the history of human rights in particular "illustrates the persistence of the nation state as the aspirational forum for humanity". During the second half of the 20th century, competing ideologies, particularly utopian ones, lost their popular legitimacy, culminating in the post-Cold War era. "It was the crisis of other utopias that allowed the very neutrality [of human rights ...] to become the condition of their success" (213). This supposed neutrality is precisely the claim that rights are recognized and that they are as much moral as political categories.

This moralism of rights, which has been adopted by the rights of nature, came into the contemporary world as a form of anti-politics. In time, though, this stance – as all anti-political ones – became untenable, because "they could not remain wholly noncommittal towards programmatic endeavors" (213). As human rights inevitably moved towards ideology, replacing other dying utopias, they were mythologized as having always existed, a claim that is patently false. Ideologically, however, its empirical falsity matters little, as ideologies must take the move towards universality in order to shore up their program. In the early 21st century, they became fully incorporated with the power of the state, a process particularly visible through humanitarian interventions, predicated on incredible violence, in order to shore up human rights. In this way, they became both "the means and object" of politics, a process which moralizes politics such that its capacity to mediate conflict is severely diminished (Douzinas 2007, 7). Or as Kelefa Sanneh (2021) argues, commenting on Jamal Green's book *How Rights Went Wrong*, "the endless search for 'fundamental' rights inevitably makes disputes [...] more intractable".

The biggest problem with moralism is that it imparts an unjustifiable confidence because one is convinced of possessing the truth. This is the danger of certainty at a time when what is needed is precisely the ability (necessarily cultivated through careful and committed practice) to navigate, and live with, uncertainty (also see Tănăsescu 2022). The moralism of the rights of nature stems directly from the moralism of human rights, a phenomenon that really came into its own when rights became tools of the state, even though they were born in opposition to it. The radical core of a universal doctrine of rights – the forging of identities around universal forms of equality – became hollowed out by their becoming ideological tools through which violence is often legitimized.

I have argued that the rights of nature cannot help but participate in the liberal rights expansion that has spawned them to begin with. It is perhaps telling that, in the extant cases with the greatest and, crucially, deepest Indigenous involvement (Te Urewera and Whanganui), rights-talk is minimized as much as possible. Particularly in Te Urewera, even the idea of personhood is minimized, and the new legal construct is mostly referred to as a "legal entity". Here, theory could help future practice by asking it to reflect more on the availability of "legal entity" as an alternative to the conundrums that personhood throws up. These conundrums will manifest when we pass from human to nature's rights, because 'nature' is the same kind of totalizing abstraction that 'humanity' is. It may never be the case that all humans belong to the category of humanity because that process of inclusion is not a merely legal one, but one of political and social economy.

Similarly, and despite the totalizing nature of the Universal Declaration of the Rights of Mother Earth, not everything will belong to the category 'nature'. Pests will continue to exist, pathogens also, viruses and undesirable animals will continue to be exterminated. It is not in the power of the law to amend this situation. But it is in its power to reflect on its conceptual vocabulary and to see how it may be complicit in certain unintended consequences.

The world of individuals hermetically sealed within their heads, where they can rationally know their interests, is the world of modernity, one that is spatially flat and whose time is that of progressive linearity or development (understood, among others, in terms of the expanding rights of the individual). This world was unknown, in Europe as well as elsewhere, before the advent of modernity, which invented it. This is not, in other words, an indigenous world, and it shares very little characteristics with it. Indigenous thinking, despite its great diversity, does not tend to be focused on binary oppositions (society/nature, individual/group, and so on), but rather tends to be relational. In relational terms, what counts as being a subject varies greatly, and the idea of the person modelled on individual, 'normal' humans is entirely absent.

Instead, the world consists of mutating relationships that give rise to various subjectivities, some more enduring than others. Crucially, it consists of alliances and groups that travel through space and time, as visible through the treatment of various embodied spaces as kin (and therefore connected to the present through genealogical lines). This treatment of non-humans and non-related humans as kin is also indicative of the relatively weak role that nativist criteria play in indigenous thinking. Belonging to a place (unlike in the colonial imagination) is not only about birth, but rather about what one *does* and therefore how one relates to a series of environmental beings. The possibility of relating to the environing world in generative ways is not an ethnic one, but an ethical one.[4]

The study of what the world consists of is known in philosophy as ontology, and indigenous ontologies, as Viveiros de Castro has argued, are not simply descriptions of one same world but rather of completely different worlds. In their interaction with colonial modernity, indigenous worlds have consistently had to "translate" themselves, that is to say to adopt and adapt to a world that is not their own. In practice, this has also meant that Indigenous People have had to adopt the terminology of rights through which to interact with the state. But, as I have argued throughout, that terminology hides the power of the state to discount those subjects that do not, for whatever reason, possess the characteristics of the desired "normal person". Today, we are living through a moment that offers new possibilities for legal pluralism and hybridization, and

---

4 Though this argument is seldom explicitly made, it is supported by philosophical explorations of some indigenous thought. For example, Anne Salmond (2017), in recounting the early history of Māori – Pakeha (white settlers) relations, shows how the first fifty or so years of contact were dominated by Māori tikanga, because Pakeha were de facto guests that did not have the demographic dominance that would later allow the rise of a settler state. In this early period, many guests became 'related' to their Māori hosts by learning the language and generally adopting tikanga. This indicates that the possibility of belonging was not primarily dictated by birth. Similarly, the ritual recitation that Māori speakers engage in before speaking publically (*whaikōrero*) can draw on all sorts of genealogical lines, most of which are not blood lines, but ones of alliance. This plasticity again lends credence to the interpretation of genealogy in non-nativist terms.

it matters greatly that this moment does not end up reproducing the power differentials that have always characterized Indigenous – state relations. This is why it is important to realize how much of a compromise legal personhood and rights are and to ask what other conceptions, stemming from other worlds, we may work with going forward.

For example, on an ontological level, Amerindian philosophies consider subjectivity (subjective experience) – not matter or material properties – to be what connects all beings. In other words, "the manifest bodily form of each species is an envelope (a "clothing") that conceals an internal humanoid form" (De Castro 2019). This deep form of anthropomorphism – literally, everything has interiority – sustains a relational ontology steeped in what Marisol de la Cadena (2010, 341) calls "earth-practices", defined as "relations for which the dominant ontological distinction between humans and nature does not work". The reason is two-fold: firstly, it is relations that are primary and, secondly, it is subjectivity that connects all beings.[5] In many Amerindian philosophies, Andean ones included, there is one humanity and there are many natures, a view that de Castro calls multinaturalism.

> "The core issue, once again, is whether humans share in common with nonhumans the body or consciousness, and by that measure, even efforts against anthropo-centrism in environmental philosophy come up naturalist: either by conferring rights only to animals developed enough to be sentient or by arguing that we are responsible for life and abiotic elements because of our physical interdependence with them" (Skafish 2016b, 79). Animist philosophies posit consciousness as the unifying substance tying all forms of life together, and therefore it throws up radically different problems than the naturalism that still informs eco-anthropocentric debates. For example, the problem of life's necessity to consume life is deeply troubling in the context of shared interiority because

5 "Other-than-humans include animals, plants and the landscape" (De la Cadena 2010, 341).

> the consumption of any flesh becomes in a sense cannibalistic, requiring careful ritualization for the transgression not to be fatal. As Descola asks in light of this analysis, "do such observations not indicate that it is high time to ask whether ecological politics can really be undertaken on the basis of nature alone, and if the actual and potential actions of other collectives might somehow be needed, and even somehow practicable, by moderns as well?" (In Skafish 2016b, 79).

In the text of the Ecuadorian Constitution, Pachamama is an indigenous other-than-human figure that erupts in the political space of the state. However, the equivalence in the constitutional text between this figure and Nature – including in the Articles that grant rights to nature – is deeply problematic, as it forces the radical potential of an indigenous led politics into the molds of modernist ontology. In particular, the constitutional text falls prey to the Western obsession with totality, visible in the rendering of Pachamama as universal Nature, Earth as such, if somewhat animated by Amerindian 'beliefs'. The Constitution manages to construct nature on the model of the human person, whereas indigenous philosophy, through its multinaturalism, universalizes the interiority of the human experience (everything has a life of its own) and the dynamism and openness of material forms (and everything changes). From this perspective, it is the concept of a stable human person (with intrinsic characteristics and values) that can be destabilized by modelling it more closely on the dynamism and fundamental openness of nature. Instead, the rights of nature in the Ecuadorian case reinforce a Western view that attaches to nature the universality which it had previously attached to human rights. The possibility of allowing indigenous ontology to disrupt the very notion of universality seems, here, partly foreclosed.

Te Urewera, out of all cases so far, comes closest to ontological mixing on an equal footing. It remains telling, however, that it is not in Te Urewera Act itself that Māori ontology takes the lead, but rather in the management plan, Te Kawa o Te Urewera. There, as discussed in Chapter 4, the very idea of the person is subverted and, instead, the focus is on relationships of reciprocity with the environing world. This world is very specific, and it is precisely that ability to pay attention to specificities and get to know them deeply that has nurtured indigenous cultures from time immemorial. This capacity has been widely lost through modernity, which is why Te Kawa lucidly speaks of the need that Tūhoe themselves have to relearn to pay attention to their specific environment. The lessons that this case has for future rights of nature practice are still to be drawn, but theoretically it has already cut a new and promising path.

I do not mean to deny the effort that Indigenous People have put into achieving greater legal pluralism. Quite the contrary, that effort needs to be recognized on its own terms, not always 'translated' into western conceptions! And if we start doing that, we begin to see how what appears as an emancipatory expansion of rights may be, from the perspective of those that have never counted as full persons under liberal conditions, a further solidification of oppressive power. The opposition of Indigenous People to the concept of the state is not only philosophical, but political as well. This can be seen through the origins of the international movement of Indigenous Peoples, which has come about both through and against international bodies such as the UN system.

Ronald Niezen (2003) argues that the notion of Indigenous Peoples was itself created through the World War II expansion and internalization of human rights discourses. There is no doubt that the international movement for Indigenous Peoples was first and foremost spearheaded by Indigenous activists themselves, but the very consciousness of a common fate at the hands of settler powers was a relatively late achievement that incentivized international cooperation among different peoples. The sedimentation of indigeneity as a category referring to particular people was created through a reiterative interaction between external gazes and internal identity formation. In other words, the process of colonization and the subsequent transformation of world order through the ascendancy of the nation state interacted decisively with indigenous societies that were routinely marginalized. This is also the case in the very creation of an international indigenous identity.

The variety of experiences within Indigenous societies is seen in the difficulty of a unified definition of what constitutes indigeneity.

Despite the lack of such a definition, several common features appear, in particular the common destruction of traditional heritage at the hands of colonial powers. Indigenous identity is united around a terrible loss. The multiplicity of indigenous positions is further unified by the "absence of centralized dogma. Its main ideas [as reflected through international fora] coalesce within a large number of micronationalism and micro-orthodoxies, each a discrete movement oriented toward small communities or regions [...]. Indigenism involves reinvigoration of the comfort and color of local traditions with the safety-in-numbers effect of a global movement" (Niezen 2013, 13).

This is to say that an international Indigenous identity is in a sense forced by the dominance of nation states both in local politics and, indisputably, on the international arena. Politically then, a wide variety of different kinds of societies have had to coalesce around an international indigeneity that, despite this necessity, itself retains a commitment to a kind of inner diversity that is radically opposed to the homogeneity, and the homogenizing force, of states. The partial adoption of rights language on the international arena is a pragmatic accommodation of dominant power relations. But a closer look at what exactly the international indigenous movement claims to want reveals that it does not consistently, or even primarily, ask for equal rights, but rather for self-determination such that the small microhistories that Niezen talks about can be given practical purchase.

That is the radical core of Indigenous Peoples claims. And that is precisely the claim that states neutralize through rights. In the case of Te Urewera, the issue of full tikanga authority was taboo, because it would lead to fears of secessionism among an overwhelming settler majority. It would also pose existential question for the unified state of New Zealand and create precedents that would risk radically transforming its shape towards unknown configurations of power sharing. The Ecuadorian constitution, for example, though widely commented upon as radical in its empowerment of Indigenous People, clearly states that "The indigenous communities, pueblos and nationalities, the afroecuatorian pueblo, the montubio pueblo and the comunas form part of the Ecuadorian State, one and indivisible" (art. 56). It is the state that is one and indivisible, and the furthest it will go in relation to colonized populations is to recognize their equal status as rights bearers. Indeed, "the greatest duty of the State consists in respecting and enforcing the respect of the rights guaranteed in the Constitution" (art.11/9).

With each successive wave of national solidification around rights expansion, different possibilities are shut out. Consider again the right to restoration that has become a staple of rights of nature theory and practice. In Andean, as well as Māori, thinking, the beings that are constituted through relations are in flux; they change and adapt to new circumstances and new relations. Therefore, it is not a 'nature out there' that is worshiped as an unchangeable form. Rather, Amerindian philosophies posit environmental relations in terms of reciprocal exchanges, as do Māori ones. Through these iterative exchanges, beings continuously mutate. It is not surprising that radically place-based philosophies would also see the world as highly dynamic, because careful observation of the world reveals precisely that fact. So, something like a right to be restored needs to at least be specified in terms of what restoration may mean. If it is taken to mean a return to a 'pre-disturbance' form (baseline restoration), this kind of right can easily be used by the state to further disempower communities, as I have already shown.

Restoration, as I have argued elsewhere (Tănăsescu 2017, 2022), needs to itself be understood in relational terms and therefore in terms that let indigenous ontology lead. Restoration in the Anthropocene can no longer be about returning to some previous state but rather about returning to meaningful relations with particular places. The recurrence of an unspecified right to restoration in different cases also encourages people to think about rights as applicable to 'untouched' places, exactly the kinds of places that colonial nations had designated as Indigenous reserves. But in a world that is increasingly urban, and in any case increasingly humanized, there is an urgent need to think about what the rights of nature may mean in those settings as well, and what a right to restoration may mean in a densely populated environment. These are all issues that will have to be ironed out in the future, but in order to do so it is important to flag them as worthy of attention to begin with.

The Rights of Nature as Representation

I have argued for some time (Tănăsescu 2013, 2016, 2020, 2021) that the rights of nature are unintelligible without thinking about them as a process of politically representing nature. A nature with rights becomes, first and foremost, a *political* subject, just like a corporation with rights does. I will not repeat the details of this argument, which can be found elsewhere. Instead, I want to sketch its importance for critically examining rights of nature and draw out some of its implications.

Formally speaking, the rights that nature may receive have to be represented by someone. But this formal requirement has no purchase whatsoever unless this representation is also institutionalized in some form. This is to say that rights of nature cannot be an end in themselves or a self-implementing solution. Simply granting rights to an entity that cannot defend them on its own is useless unless the necessary aspect of representation is given a practical outline. This is partly why, in the cases of Ecuador and Bolivia, the representation of nature is prone to partisan abuse: There is no mechanism of representation mandated by these laws, so anyone can bend them to their particular interest. Similarly, in the Indian cases, the mechanism of representation – affording guardianship to local authorities – was so shoddy that the putative representatives themselves refused to do the job.

Focusing on representative arrangements makes it possible to ask why rights are granted to nature in any particular case. The orthodox answer is that they are granted, in every case, in order to achieve environmental protection. This should ring hollow by now. I don't doubt advocates' good intentions, but I think I have shown in detail how these do not translate into guarantees of environmentally friendly results. Instead, I have demonstrated that the rights of nature are inevitably intertwined with pre-existing power relations. Thinking about them as mechanisms of representation allows this aspect of power to come to the fore and therefore to determine how laws are written. If, indeed, they are to be written for environmental protection, then this needs to be carefully thought out in terms of who has the moral and political authority to oversee such protection.

In the most innovative cases so far, Te Urewera and Whanganui, environmental protection was not the main motivator. In both cases, classic environmental institutions, like conservation ministries, were sidelined and power given to other groups that may or may not choose similar goals. From a Māori perspective this makes sense, because from their ontological standpoint there is no such thing as pure 'environmental protection', but rather the systematic encouragement of destructive, or regenerative, relationships. The kind of fortress conservation that has been a staple of modernist environmentalism should be actively questioned. Rights of nature will inevitably work to empower certain groups over others. The choice of which groups, and for what reasons, is crucial.[6]

Rights as representative arrangements steeped in pre-existing power relations allows us to find other allies that may not themselves appeal to the concept of rights, or that of legal personality. For example, the idea of commons (or, as it is also known in the literature, commoning – therefore putting the accent on the *process* of achieving commons) is present in many forms and in many different cultures. The basic idea, as developed most famously by Elinor Ostrom (1990), is that lands have, in many cultures and in many places, been managed as common goods. Customary law has recognized and enforced this common good status, which always passes through a series of community-determined rules of conduct that ensure the sustainable long-term use of resources (also see Bollier and Helfrich 2019).

The practice of commoning can be seen as a useful bridge between a-modern ontologies in parts of the world that have been put, by modernity itself, in stark opposition to each other. As Tanas and

6 It is important to realize that choosing to *not* make this choice – and, for example, allowing for universal and wide standing – does not sidestep power relations. Instead, it relegates power to the already most powerful.

Gutwirth (2021) argue, the Whanganui case has definite similarities to the law of commons in Sardinia, Italy (*usi civici*). Other such customary laws exist throughout Europe, and throughout the world, without relying on liberal rights at all. Focusing on the importance (indeed, inevitability) of representation allows us to also see practices such as commoning as important allies that may work, in some cases, together with rights of nature. For example, legal entity status may work in order to bring commoners' lands into a form of representation that empowers local communities. But in this case also, the use of the environment is fundamental, and therefore these kinds of arrangements will often not conform to an ecocentric environmental agenda.

Another potential ally is the much-hated idea of corporate personhood. In particular, the corporate structure that separates ownership (vested in the legal fiction of the corporation itself) from management and governance may also work very well in some cases to solve ownership disputes. In Te Urewera, for example, Katherine Sanders (2018) argued that this is exactly what happened. The rights of nature, as minimalist legal entity status, in fact gave ownership of Te Urewera to Te Urewera itself, which now resembles a corporate structure with a board (ensuring governance) and shareholders (enjoying the benefits generated by Te Urewera). It may be that, because of this structure, Te Urewera can become an important political and economic actor, like corporations have through the granting of their legal personality. Because of this, it matters even more who sits on the board and who gets to determine government arrangements. In other words, it matters even more who represents Te Urewera.

This awareness of rights as representation is obvious when looking at the details of Te Urewera and the Whanganui cases. As I have explored in Chapter 4, these are extremely focused on setting up a democratic process of representation that allows Māori autonomy to come forward in previously suppressed ways. Precisely because these are essentially political arrangements, they will also be temporary and prone to changing. This is to say that the Māori fight for greater autonomy is not over with these arrangements, but rather recast on a basis that grants them more power. All rights of nature are political in this sense. Acknowledging this fact allows us to work with it and to construct laws that may also have the desired effects in practice. Importantly, it also allows practitioners to question the purpose of nature's rights actively and to perhaps find new purposes that it can ally with.

The Rights of Nature as Movement

The diversity of theory and practice that I have presented may or may not warrant the claim that the rights of nature constitute a movement. To be sure, homogeneity is not the hallmark of a movement; but it is worth examining more closely the claim that the disparate cases this book has surveyed, as well as others it has not, are all part of the same movement for rights. Questioning this claim is important in order to safeguard diversity and multiplicity wherever it is threatened. There seems to be an increasing capture of diversity for the purpose of molding it into ecotheological orthodoxy and liberal rights expansionism. This is why it is important to be clear about what it may mean to claim that there is a movement, and how that claim may allow, or not, a diversity of views to thrive.

Claiming to be a movement may mean different things. At the most straightforward level, it simply indicates a growing trend, a move towards something, in this case towards rights of nature. At this level of analysis, it is undeniable that these rights are a growing trend. Besides this strictly linguistic definition of movement, there is a vast literature on what are generally called social movements that can be helpful here. I suspect that when advocates claim to be part of a movement, they also mean part of a *social* movement. This interpretation is warranted by the actions and priorities of certain key organizations, while also being doubtful in some of its senses.

In the relevant literature, there is no commonly accepted definition of what constitutes a social movement. This doesn't mean that anything goes. Instead, the lack of a foolproof definition reflects the malleability and largely informal nature of such movements. Marco Diani, one of the leading scholars in that field, speaks of social movements as having boundaries drawn by "processes of mutual recognition whereby social actors recognize different elements as part of the same collective experience and identify some criteria that differentiate them from the rest" (in van Stekelenburg et al 2013). However, this does not mean that a social movement is formed by formal interests that may be in common between different organizations. As he points out, an organization for the protection of birds need not also be part of the environmental movement unless, of course, it has specific ties (organizational and identity-based) with that movement.

Following from the above, the overall narrative within which a particular event, or a particular organization, is embedded, is extremely important for deciding whether something is a movement. Diani gives the example of a protest against industrial pollution in a working-class area. He points out that it could be part of an environmental movement, a class struggle, or a not-in-my-back-yard movement. It all depends on the overall narrative within which it is inscribed and the goals and policies that the narrative endorses and makes possible. This means that it is crucially important to see how different cases are presented, and by which organizations, in order to assess if a movement is indeed taking shape.

Social movements rely on interorganizational networks that present an encompassing narrative and set goals to be pursued. However, unlike in formal organizations, movements are largely informal, and a strong identity component is present. This also implies that movements can be very fluid, change over time, and include a great heterogeneity of views. These may splinter, in the course of time, into separate movements, or else continue co-existing within an overall grander narrative. But if we speak of a movement, the literature tends to agree, we are also speaking of "networks of informal interaction between a plurality of individuals, groups and/or organizations, engaged in cultural or political conflicts, on the basis of shared collective identities" (Diani 1992).

As we have seen earlier, the main rights of nature organizations have indeed been engaged in largely informal interactions that have been decisive for several cases, key among which the Ecuadorian constitution. That experience and its wide publicity have also popularized nature's rights as an idea and diffused it widely. However, that kind of diffusion does not necessarily make a movement since the recipients of the idea (as in the Colombian and Indian cases) may or may not share organizational networks and/or collective identities. What is certain is that important organizations are putting a lot of effort into expanding their base and transforming the organization of rights of nature from an elite-driven enterprise into a grassroots one.

Early cases, and especially the most publicized ones, like Ecuador and Bolivia, have been elite driven. In these cases, political and intellectual elites had already decided on a preferred course of action, which was then implemented when a window of opportunity opened up (Kingdon and Stano 1984). CELDF, the most influential organization in the actual writing of legislation to date,[7] has also driven community initiatives for rights of nature at municipal levels in the United States. Here, too, there has always been a pre-determined goal (of reaching rights of nature), and an increasing effort to diffuse this goal widely and gather community support. This meant that CELDF has been putting a lot of effort into tying community rights, human rights, minority rights and nature's rights into a logical and seamless web.

Whether the rights of nature conform to the scholarly definition of a social movement may, in itself, be of little interest. What I want to show through this short foray into that literature is that there are characteristics that these rights share with social movements, and others that they don't. For example, not all rights for nature have emanated out of an international policy network. The New Zealand cases, for instance, have had a parallel development and, indeed, share little of the ecotheological history.[8] In terms of the identity of people participating in rights of nature advocacy, this also varies widely, and at this point it is hard to say whether there is such a thing as a shared identity at all. If anything, considering

7 Given its composition, the new Center for Democratic and Environmental Rights (CDER) may as well become equally influential in the future.

8 This does not mean that important actors in the NZ cases had no idea of their history and practice elsewhere. For example, Morris and Ruru (2010) explicitly follow Cristopher Stone's analysis of legal personality and draw an explicit parallel between that Western legal concept and Māori tikanga.

rights of nature as a movement in this particular historical moment would require a definition of movements as quite encompassing of heterogeneity of identities.

The most important question that arises out of this discussion, as far as I'm concerned, is what the grander narrative that organizes the movement is. If we take our cue from the dominant organizations, then this narrative is undeniably the liberal theory of rights and its expansion. These organizations promote this particular narrative while incorporating all possible cases into it even though there is great diversity of practice. This can be both a tool for further expansion and one for policing how rights of nature may develop. Whether or not advocates in new and different cases subscribe to the ecotheology of rights is important in assessing what kind of movement is burgeoning. Currently, a look at the resources pages displayed by the most important organizations reveals that they list no critical titles, even though these exist. This can be a deep problem for the creation of an inclusive movement.

Some of the theoretical commitments of ecotheology, including the idea that the rights of nature are but the next step in the expanding circle of moral concern, may restrict how future cases develop. If Te Urewera would have indeed developed as part of an international movement, it would have granted Tūhoe the status of guardians, therefore restricting the ways in which Māori jurisprudential traditions may influence current and future governance practices. Other potential innovations would benefit from a wider opening within the growing trend towards rights divergence, and for self-reflection and questioning. The kind of questioning I have in mind is already present in cases that are currently being theoretically elaborated, in preparation for future practical deployment.

For example, a recent article (RiverOfLife et al 2020) proposes that Martuwarra river in Australia be designated a legal person, but it does so in a way that puts indigenous jurisprudence front and center and therefore builds yet another path for the rights of nature to travel through. It proposes, among other innovations, that the right to life be interpreted as connected to the crime of ecocide, itself connected to the internationally recognized crime of genocide. It convincingly argues that ecocide is a way towards genocide, a claim that comes directly out of Indigenous experiences of dispossession.[9] But it does not make this argument based on the liberal expansionism of rights, and this matters greatly in diversifying the theoretical and practical toolkit that legal innovation can propose in the future.

On the strength of the social movement literature, rights of nature both are and aren't a movement at this stage in their development. If it is to become a truly inclusive one, then the organizations currently dominating the field need to adopt, in my view, a much more critical stance towards the orthodoxy that they themselves are helping build. Any movement is as good as the vigilance that allows it to stave off the almost inevitable ossification of its positions. Defending against this inherent danger will allow the rights of nature to evolve and perhaps to overcome their uncomfortable alliance with liberal rights orthodoxy.

---

9 As Philip Sands showed in East West Street (2016), by uncovering the origins of genocide, this internationally recognized crime stood in contrast to the contemporaneously created "crimes against humanity". The former applies to groups, while the latter to individuals. In this sense, crimes against humanity comes closer to the rights-driven approach explored here, whereas genocide/ecocide would apply to specific groups/biomes. This distinction is worth pursuing further, especially as the crime of ecocide is poised to become increasingly important in international law. Ecocide may well offer a way towards condemning ecological crimes without heavily relying on the category of rights.

Chapter VII: Conclusions
The Problem of Good Intentions

An introductory book cannot help but gloss over many details that more thorough scholarly engagement would be sensitive to. But if it succeeds, it manages to focus on strains and connections that may not be visible when looking too closely at individual cases. An introduction should straddle the perilous border between generality and particularity and show the many ways in which they connect. Indeed, it should show how abstraction is the infrastructure of practice, and practice the fodder of abstraction.

I set the rights of nature within the context of the inseparability of liberal rights expansion on the one hand and growth-fueled development on the other. I argued that the glue that holds these apparently divergent movements together is the power of the (often colonial or neo-colonial) nation state. Because of this, one of the most significant contributions of the rights of nature so far has been the opening up of spaces that subjugated people can use in order to inject radically different legal and philosophical traditions into the Western mainstream. On the other hand, the insistence on rights risks propagating liberal orthodoxy further, unwittingly accelerating the Great Acceleration.

Erin O'Donnell and colleagues (2020), in an article analyzing indigenous involvement in nature's rights, very helpfully separate the cases seen so far into two different kinds: cases focused on Nature and on versions of the right to life (broadly, what I have called ecotheology); and cases focused on particular places and on legal personality only. As the authors explain, legal personality as such gives rise to three different rights, namely the right to hold property

(Te Urewera owns itself), the right to enter and enforce contracts (as a separate legal entity), and the right to sue and be sued (legal standing). The cases of Ecuador and Bolivia have become the emblematic ones for ecotheological rights, while the cases of Aotearoa New Zealand are paradigmatic of the focus on legal personality itself.

O'Donnell and her co-authors also point out, as I have, that the first kind of rights are also moral rights, whereas legal personality is morally agnostic. In the first case, advocates have stressed the opposition between being a thing and being a person. The argument is that those two kinds of beings are incompatible: if nature is a thing (a resource), it cannot be a person, and vice versa. The second kind of rights for nature show this to be a false premise in practice (it had already been shown to be false in theory; see Chapter 2): Te Urewera is both a legal entity and a thing that is owned by the legal entity. These kinds of constructions are familiar to Western law, which routinely aggregates interests into fictitious 'persons' that have different roles in different circumstances.

The minimal grant of legal entity status can, in theory, accomplish a much more focused application of the law to places and allow for representative arrangements that integrate and give practical power to a-modern ontologies. This is incredibly important, as it opens up spaces of innovation. I have argued that there is still a long way to go before a truly consistent indigenous leadership is allowed within the centers of Western legal and political power, but what O'Donnell et al refer to as 'ecological jurisprudence (also see Bosselmann 2012) leaves much more room for this to happen than does the ecotheological Earth jurisprudence that I have analyzed. Though this is not currently the case, ecological law shows promise in potentially side-stepping the issue of rights and its liberal expansionism in favor of allowing radically different ontologies to propose alternative arrangements.

This split within rights of nature theory and practice is thankfully becoming more widely recognized, which should help practice tremendously. What still needs due recognition is the outsized influence that ecotheology still has, particularly in the diffusion of ideas. On the one hand, this can be seen (see Chapter 4) by the almost universal adoption of the term 'guardianship' to characterize the political arrangements inaugurated by Te Urewera and Whanganui. I have myself used this term without realizing that, in doing so, I was unwittingly brushing over the radical novelty that Māori involvement in these cases had proposed (Tănăsescu 2016). A "human face" is not a guardian, but something more like a representative, and once we ask *what kind* of representative that is, a door is opened towards a world in which Māori can lead, explaining what that may mean and showing it in practice.

Similarly, the influence of the Aotearoa cases on the Colombian and Indian ones has been widely recognized. But, because of the capture of the New Zealand cases by ecotheology (through, among other tropes, the one of guardianship), judges in Colombia and India only superficially travelled the path opened by Māori ontologies. Instead, they ended up passing laws that are much closer to Earth jurisprudence and only superficially tied to indigenous ontologies. This is why the dominance of ecotheology in the diffusion of rights for nature globally is so important to challenge; it homogenizes possibilities into a globalist blend of moralist rights that are highly vulnerable.

The movement for rights of nature, inasmuch as there is one single movement at all, has to start taking the real variety of cases and theoretical orientations into account. It may be that, in doing so, the very idea of *rights* needs to be rethought. It may also be that the *purpose* of these rights needs to be much more actively interrogated (see Tănăsescu 2021b). The Indian and Colombian cases seemed to think that rights are for environmental protection, a claim that I have shown to come out of the moral/legal confusion propagated by ecotheology. On the other hand, the Aotearoa cases show clearly political purposes, with no primary concern for environmental protection as such, in part because they are not predicated on a separation of humans and environments.

I don't mean to imply that in New Zealand a perfect 'inclusion' of Māori thinking has been achieved. I have presented a much more nuanced view of this in Tănăsescu (2020a). Instead, I do want to suggest that those cases cut a new path, one that has much greater potential for much greater inclusion. In Australia the Martuwarra/Fitzroy river is currently being considered as a candidate for legal entity status, and crucially this is being done in open dialogue between First Law and settler law. The idea of legal entity status still needs refining, and I have also argued that we may be better served by abandoning the idea of person or personality altogether, focusing on entities instead. This can allow a more important role for a-modern philosophies and legal practices, as 'entity' is completely neutral in moral terms. It can therefore defend itself against the liberal rights expansionism that the state is so comfortable with.

Cases of rights of nature are proliferating at an expanding rate. In Bangladesh, the supreme court declared Turag river, as well as all other rivers in the country, to be legal persons (Islam and O'Donnell 2020). Lake Eerie, in the United States, was briefly granted rights before the decision was struck down in higher courts. The Universal Declaration of the Rights of Mother Earth may well one day be adopted, and its example has already emboldened the creation of an International Rights of Nature Tribunal. Increasingly, international media report on new and exciting cases: a lagoon in Spain, a wetland in Florida, all aquatic ecosystems in Europe. This proliferation makes the work of critical assessment ever more urgent, such that orthodoxy does not set in and rights expansionism is not unreflectively given an unexpected boost, just when a world of Total Production seems to be imminent.

*

The rights of nature are too often presented as achieving environmental protection and moral enlightenment. I have argued against this kind of totality thinking throughout. If we abandon it and instead focus on the multiplicity of struggles, and on the possibility of wide and regenerative cohabitation outside Western moral frameworks, then we start seeing all sorts of allies that were not visible before.

For example, by focusing on representation as a very salient aspect of including environments in political (and legal) processes, Bruno Latour has famously proposed the idea of a parliament of things.[1] Following up on this idea, a diverse group of people in the Netherlands have put together an Embassy of the North Sea, which is supposed to understand whether there is something like the North Sea that can speak in politically intelligible speech (also see Lambooy et al 2019, who make the case of legal personality for the Wadden sea). Tellingly, their exercise starts with listening, and incorporates art as a fundamental part of both listening and speaking processes (after all, the concept of representation cannot be properly thought without dialogue with art; see Tănăsescu 2014). In other words, this initiative recuperates the need to pay close attention that has been all but obliterated by the homogenous spaces of modern development.

Similarly, the practice and theory of commoning can be an excellent ally, and one that can put into dialogue a-modern traditions that do not have to respect the colonial center-periphery, mainstream-exotic dichotomies. But if the rights of nature continue to be dominated by the call to awaken to the moral personality of Mother Earth, all of these other tendencies cannot really be seen as allies. The parliament of 'things' doesn't fail to see the personhood of nature, but rather tries to imagine worlds governed beyond modernist dichotomies. Similarly, commoners have, and have always had, a wide variety of ontologically derived practices. What matters is that these be regenerative of socio-ecological practices, as opposed to inherently consumptive and destructive.

The expression *rights of nature* is catchy and concise and therefore very amenable to travelling far and wide. But it also risks hiding orientations that are not centered around rights, yet use these selectively, like the cases granting minimal entity status and focusing on representative arrangements. I am not sure that the burgeoning Rights of Nature international trademark can take a step back from rights and recognize their inherent problems. As Douzinas argues, "a society where individual rights with their adversarial culture have become the main moral source can survive only with the help of criminal law, the police force and extensive surveillance"

1 For the use of this idea in an interpretation of the Colombian case, see Cagüeñas et al (2020).

(Gearty and Douzinas 2012, 64). A society where everything starts having rights will inevitably have to weigh them against each other, and it will generally be the most powerful that prevail. The police and extensive surveillance seem inevitable.

Equally problematic is the reliance on the totalizing figure of Nature. In practice, this risks focusing rights on exceptional environments or on a new kind of conservation agenda that can continue to exclude local communities from using their environment. The urban environment is almost absent from the rights of nature; this is a mistake that will need to be corrected. In order to do so, the right to restoration needs to be thoroughly rethought, in ways that empower local communities to develop regenerative relations outside of the problems that baselines impose. It also needs to be insulated against the capacity of the state to use it selectively for extractive purposes.

The label "ecological jurisprudence" may offer a good way out of the conundrums that enshrining rights and Nature into the very name of the growing movement throws up. It can also help move away from the nation state as the focus of environmental governance. Bosselmann (2015) argues that "as long as innovative ideas are exclusively derived from what states are willing to support, no genuine progress will be made" (268). He shows that legal innovation needs to focus much more on tools that can be used against the state, not on ones that the most powerful actors are already comfortable with. In other words, we need as much political as legal innovation, and the two have to work together in order to make a substantive difference. In the New Zealand cases, for example, the settler state was more comfortable giving rights to nature than to the Indigenous populations (like full property rights over their lands and waters). The idea of self-ownership for Te Urewera, though incredibly useful in many ways, was nonetheless a way to *not* vest ownership in Tūhoe.

The question of the purpose (what do we want to achieve, and who is this we?) of rights and/or legal personality should be actively and critically asked. It is not enough to assume that rights of nature are for environmental protection. Inasmuch as environmental protection is the goal, an active engagement with the colonial history of conservation should be pursued. If local community empowerment is the goal, then care should be taken to provide for the appropriate political infrastructure. If both of these goals are pursued simultaneously, then the question of how to do so remains an open one and each case will probably have a different answer.

But thinking that rights are a protection per se and that ecocentrism vs anthropocentrism is *the* way to think about legal and political pluralism shackles the imagination and risks being damaging. Instead, the opening that the explosion of rights of nature cases has created can be used to free the political and legal imagination to think critically beyond rights and beyond well-trodden binaries. For example, it may be worth considering how the law can help scale back the monopoly that state power has over setting economic and social goals. The movement for degrowth (D'Alisa et al 2014, Demaria and Kothari 2017) is yet to be allied with legal innovation, but it may hold exciting promises by writing degrowth goals into legal personality arrangements and by providing the appropriate infrastructure. Similarly, the infrastructure for alternatives to development needs to be thought out in detail, as it is not enough to proclaim grand goals that can be easily accommodated to progressive neo-extractivism.

In the Cambridge Companion to Human Rights Law, Costas Douzinas opens his chapter on rights jurisprudence with the following cautionary tale: "when, in 1983, I ran the first-ever human rights course in my Law School only four brave and idealistic students registered, making me almost abandon the exercise. I told these pioneers that human rights are the conscience of law, practiced by a few idealistic lawyers and invoked by dissidents and rebels. How different things look today. If only thirty years ago rights were the repressed conscience of the profession, they have now become its dominant rhetoric. […] The dissident pioneers have become the established majority, the repressed idealism dominant consciousness, the protest ruling ideology" (Gearty and Douzinas 2012, 57). It would be a momentous loss of opportunity if, thirty years from now, the rights of nature have become the new mainstream, the domain of "the established majority". Defending against this possibility goes through political as much as legal innovation. Refusing orthodoxy in favor of new and unprecedented alliances is the moral task ahead.

Bibliography

Abram, D. (2012). The spell of the sensuous: Perception and language in a more-than-human world. Vintage.

Acosta, A., Gudynas, E., Martínez, E., & Vogel, J. (2009). Dejar el crudo en tierra o la búsqueda del paraíso perdido. Elementos para una propuesta política y económica para la Iniciativa de no explotación del crudo del ITT. Polis. Revista Latinoamericana, (23).

Acosta, A. (2010). Toward the universal declaration of rights of nature: thoughts for action. AFESE journal, 24(1).

Acosta, A. (2013). El Buen Vivir: Sumak Kawsay, una oportunidad para imaginar otros mundos. Barcelona: Icaria.

Alley, K. D. (2019). River goddesses, personhood and rights of nature: implications for spiritual ecology. Religions, 10(9), 502.

Antony, L. M. (2000). Natures and norms. Ethics, 111(1), 8-36.

Arstein-Kerslake, A. (2017). Restoring voice to people with cognitive disabilities. Cambridge University Press.

Bales, K., Trodd, Z., & Williamson, A. K. (2009). Modern slavery: The secret world of 27 million people. Oneworld Publications Limited.

Belgrave, Michael (2013). Historical Frictions: Māori claims and reinvented histories. Auckland: Auckland University Press.

Berkes, F. (2017). Sacred ecology. Routledge.

Berti, D. (2021). Ritual Presence and Legal Persons. Deities and the Law in India. In Anne de Sales and Marie Lecomte-Tilouine (eds.), Encounters with the Invisible. Revisiting Possession in the Himalayas in its Material and Narrative Aspects, in press.

Berry, T. (2011). The great work: Our way into the future. Crown.

Berry, W. (2003). Citizenship Papers, Berkley: Counterpoint Press.

Binney, J. (2010). Stories without end: Essays 1975–2010. Bridget Williams Books.

Binney, J. (2009). Encircled lands: Te Urewera, 1820-1921. Bridget Williams Books.

Bollier, D., & Helfrich, S. (2019). Free, fair, and alive: The insurgent power of the commons. New Society Publishers.

Bosselmann, K. (2012). The way forward: Governance for ecological integrity. In Reconciling Human Existence with Ecological Integrity (pp. 345-358). Routledge.

Bosselmann, K. (2015). Earth governance: trusteeship of the global commons. Edward Elgar Publishing.

Bourke, J. (2011). What it means to be human: Historical reflections from the 1800s to the Present. Catapult.

Boyd, D. R. (2017). The rights of nature: A legal revolution that could save the world. ECW Press.

Büscher, B., Sullivan, S., Neves, K., Igoe, J., & Brockington, D. (2012). Towards a synthesized critique of neoliberal biodiversity conservation. Capitalism nature socialism, 23(2), 4-30.

Büscher, B., & Fletcher, R. (2020). The conservation revolution: radical ideas for saving nature beyond the Anthropocene. Verso Trade.

Cagüeñas, D., Orrego, M. I. G., & Rasmussen, S. (2020). El Atrato y sus guardianes: imaginación ecopolítica para hilar nuevos derechos. Revista Colombiana de Antropología, 56(2), 169-196.

Calzadilla, P. V., & Kotzé, L. J. (2018). Living in harmony with nature? A critical appraisal of the rights of Mother Earth in Bolivia. Transnational Environmental Law, 7(3), 397-424.

Calzadilla, P. V. (2019). A Paradigm Shift in Courts' View on Nature: The Atrato River and Amazon Basin Cases in Colombia. Law Env't & Dev. J., 15, xiii.

Campbell, T. (2011). Rights: A critical introduction. Taylor & Francis.

Centro de Estudios para la Justicia Social 'Tierra Digna' and Others v President of the Republic and Others No T-622 of 2016, Corte Constitucional [Constitutional Court], Sala Sexta de Revision [Sixth Chamber] (Colombia) (10 November 2016) 137 (Tierra Digna).

Chakrabarty, D. (2009a). The climate of history: Four theses. Critical inquiry, 35(2), 197-222.

Chakrabarty, D. (2009b). Provincializing Europe. Princeton University Press.

Chakrabarty, D. (2018). The Crises of Civilization: Exploring Global and Planetary Histories. Oxford University Press.

Charbonnier, P. (2020). Abondance et liberté. La Découverte.

Ciepley, D. (2013). Beyond public and private: Toward a political theory of the corporation. American Political Science Review, 139-158.

Clark, C., Emmanouil, N., Page, J., & Pelizzon, A. (2018). Can You Hear the Rivers Sing: Legal Personhood, Ontology, and the Nitty-Gritty of Governance. Ecology LQ, 45, 787.

Colas, G. (2012). Penser l'icône en Inde ancienne. Brepols.

Constantinescu, Ş., & Tănăsescu, M. (2018). Simplifying a deltaic labyrinth: anthropogenic imprint on river deltas. Revista de Geomorfologie, 20(1), 66-78.

Crutzen, P. J. (2002, November). The "anthropocene". In Journal de Physique IV (Proceedings) (Vol. 12, No. 10, pp. 1-5). EDP sciences.

Crutzen, P. J. (2006). The "anthropocene". In Earth system science in the anthropocene (pp. 13-18). Springer, Berlin, Heidelberg.

Crutzen, P. J., & Stoermer, E. F. (2000). The anthropocene IGBP newsletter, 41. Royal Swedish Academy of Sciences, Stockholm, Sweden.

Cullinan, C. (2011). Wild law. Siber Ink.

D'Alisa, G., Demaria, F., & Kallis, G. (Eds.). (2014). Degrowth: a vocabulary for a new era. Routledge.

Daly, E. (2012). The Ecuadorian exemplar: the first ever vindications of constitutional rights of nature. Rev. Eur. Comp. & Int'l Envtl. L., 21, 63.

Das Acevedo, D. (2018). Pause for Thought: Supreme Court's Verdict on Sabarimala. Economic & Political Weekly, 53(43), 12.

Davies, M. (2012). Persons, property, and community. feminists@law, 2(2).

Debaise, D. (2017). Nature as event: The lure of the possible. Duke University Press.

de La Bellacasa, M. P. (2017). Matters of care: Speculative ethics in more than human worlds (Vol. 41). U of Minnesota Press.

de Castro, E. V. (1996). Images of nature and society in Amazonian ethnology. Annual review of Anthropology, 25(1), 179-200.

de Castro, E. V. (2014a). Cannibal metaphysics. Trans. Peter Skafish. Minneapolis: Univocal.

De Castro, E. V. (2014b). Perspectivisme et multinaturalisme en Amérique indigène. Journal des anthropologues. Association française des anthropologues, (138-139), 161-181.

De Castro, E. V. (2019). Exchanging perspectives: the transformation of objects into subjects in Amerindian ontologies. Common knowledge, 25(1-3), 21-42.

De la Cadena, M. (2015). Earth beings: Ecologies of practice across Andean worlds. Duke University Press.

Demaria, F., & Kothari, A. (2017). The Post-Development Dictionary agenda: paths to the pluriverse. Third World Quarterly, 38(12), 2588-2599.

Descola, P. (2013). Beyond nature and culture. University of Chicago Press.

Descola, P. (2014). Modes of being and forms of predication. Hau: Journal of Ethnographic Theory 4(1), 271-280.

Diani, M. (1992). The concept of social movement. The sociological review, 40(1), 1-25.

Douzinas, C. (2000). The end of human rights: Critical thought at the turn of the century. Bloomsbury Publishing.

Douzinas, C. (2007). Human rights and empire: the political philosophy of cosmopolitanism. Routledge.

Drury, W. H., & Nisbet, I. C. (1973). Succession. Journal of the Arnold arboretum, 54(3), 331-368.

Drury Jr, W. H. (1998). Chance and change: ecology for conservationists. Univ of California Press.

Duffy, R., Massé, F., Smidt, E., Marijnen, E., Büscher, B., Verweijen, J., … & Lunstrum, E. (2019). Why we must question the militarisation of conservation. Biological Conservation, 232, 66-73.

Elliot, R. (2008). Faking nature: the ethics of environmental restoration. Routledge.

Ellis, E. C., Gauthier, N., Goldewijk, K. K., Bird, R. B., Boivin, N., Díaz, S., ... & Watson, J. E. (2021). People have shaped most of terrestrial nature for at least 12,000 years. Proceedings of the National Academy of Sciences, 118(17).

Erueti, A. (2017). Conceptualising indigenous rights in Aotearoa New Zealand, New Zealand Universities Law Review (27), 715-743.

Estupiñán Achury, L., Storini, C., Martínez Dalmau, R., & Carvalho Dantas, F. A. D. (2018). La naturaleza como sujeto de derechos en el constitucionalismo democrático.

Finlayson, C. Address to Tūhoe – Crown Settlement Day in Taneatua, 23 August 2014. Available at https://www.beehive.govt.nz/speech/address-tuhoe-crown-settlement-day-taneatua

Fitz-Henry, E. (2018). Challenging Corporate "Personhood": Energy Companies and the "Rights" of Non-Humans. PoLAR: Political and Legal Anthropology Review, 41(S1), 85-102.

Fukuyama, F. (1989). The end of history?. The national interest, (16), 3-18.

Gearty, C., & Douzinas, C. (Eds.). (2012). The Cambridge companion to human rights law. Cambridge University Press.

Grear, A. (2013). Law's Entities: Complexity, Plasticity and Justice. Jurisprudence, 4(1), 76-101.

Green, J. (2021). How Rights Went Wrong: Why Our Obsession with Rights is Tearing America Apart. New York: Houghton Mifflin Harcourt.

Gudynas, E. (2009). Diez tesis urgentes sobre el nuevo extractivismo. Contextos y demandas bajo el progresismo sudamericano actual. In VV AA (ed), Extractivismo, política y sociedad, Quito: CAAP y CLAES.

Higgins, R. (2019). Ko te mana tuatoru, ko te mana motuhake. In Hickfor and Jones (eds), Indigenous Peoples and the State, London: Routledge, 129-139.

Hohfeld, W. N. (1917). Fundamental legal conceptions as applied in judicial reasoning. The Yale Law Journal, 26(8), 710-770.

Islam, M. S., & O'Donnell, E. (2020). Legal rights for the Turag: rivers as living entities in Bangladesh. Asia Pacific Journal of Environmental Law, 23(2), 160-177.

Jackson, M. (1992). The Treaty and the Word: The Colonization of Māori Philosophy. In Oddie, Graham and Perret, Roy (eds.), Justice, Ethics and Nez Zealand Society, p.1-11. Auckland: Oxford University Press.

Jones, C. (2016). New Treaty, new tradition: reconciling New Zealand and Māori law. UBC Press.

Katz, E. (2009). The big lie: human restoration of nature. Readings in the Philosophy of Technology, 443.

Kauffman, C.M., Martin, P.L. (2017a). Can Rights of Nature Make Development More Sustainable? Why Some Ecuadorian lawsuits Succeed and Others Fail. World Development (92), 130-142.

Kauffman, C.M., Martin, P.L. (2017b). Comparing Rights of Nature Laws in the US, Ecuador, and New Zealand: Evolving Strategies in the Battle Between Environmental Protection and "Development". In International Studies Association Annual Conference.

Kawharu, M. (2010). Environment as a marae locale. Māori and the Environment: Kaitiaki, 221-237.

Kingdon, J. W., & Stano, E. (1984). Agendas, alternatives, and public policies (Vol. 45, pp. 165-169). Boston: Little, Brown.

Kotzé, L. J., & Villavicencio Calzadilla, P. (2017). Somewhere between rhetoric and reality: Environmental constitutionalism and the rights of nature in Ecuador. TEL, 6, 401.

Kowii, A. (2009). El sumak kawsay. Aportes Andinos, 28, 2011.

Kurki, V. AJ. (2019). Theory of Legal Personhood. Oxford: Oxford University Press.

Lalander, R. (2014). Rights of nature and the indigenous peoples in Bolivia and Ecuador: A Straitjacket for Progressive Development Politics?. Iberoamerican Journal of Development Studies, 3(2), 148-172.

Lambooy, T., van de Venis, J., & Stokkermans, C. (2019). A case for granting legal personality to the Dutch part of the Wadden Sea. Water International, 44(6-7), 786-803.

Latour, B. (2004). Politics of nature. Harvard University Press.

Latour, B. (2017). Facing Gaia: Eight lectures on the new climatic regime. John Wiley & Sons.

Leimbacher, J. (1988). Die Rechte der Natur. Base und Frankfurt am Main: Helbing & Lichtenhahn.

Macpherson, E. (2019). Indigenous Water Rights in Law and Regulation. Cambridge: Cambridge University Press.

Macpherson, E., & Clavijo Ospina, F. C. (2020). The pluralism of river rights in Aotearoa, New Zealand and Colombia.

Macpherson, E. (2021a). The (Human) Rights of Nature: A Comparative Study of Emerging Legal Rights for Rivers and Lakes in the United States of America and Mexico. Duke Environmental Law and Policy, ...

Macpherson, E. (2021b). Ecosystem rights and the Anthropocene in Australia and Aotearoa New Zealand, in Amirante and Bagni (eds), Environmental Constitutionalism in the Anthropocene: Values, Principles, Actions. London: Routledge.

Malm, A. (2016). Fossil Capital. London: Verso.

Margil, M. (2014). Building an international movement for rights of nature. In Wild Law—In Practice (pp. 149-160). Routledge.

Mitchell, T. (2011). Carbon Democracy. London: Verso.

Morgan-Foster, J. (2005). Third generation rights: what Islamic law can teach the international human rights movement. Yale Hum. Rts. & Dev. LJ, 8, 67.

Morris, J. D., & Ruru, J. (2010). Giving voice to rivers: legal personality as a vehicle for recognising indigenous peoples'relationships to water?. Australian Indigenous Law Review, 14(2), 49-62.

Moore, J. W. (2017). The Capitalocene, Part I: on the nature and origins of our ecological crisis. The Journal of peasant studies, 44(3), 594-630.

Moore, J. W. (2018). The Capitalocene Part II: accumulation by appropriation and the centrality of unpaid work/energy. The Journal of Peasant Studies, 45(2), 237-279.

Moyn, S. (2012). The last utopia: human rights in history. Harvard University Press.

Naffine, N. (2003). Who are law's persons? From Cheshire cats to responsible subjects. The Modern Law Review, 66(3), 346-367.

Naffine, N. (2009). Law's meaning of life: Philosophy, religion, Darwin and the legal person. Bloomsbury Publishing.

Naffine, N. (2011). Liberating the legal person. Canadian Journal of Law and Society, 26(1), 193-203.

Naffine, N. (2017) 'Legal Persons as Abstractions: The Extrapolation of Persons from the Male Case' in Visa AJ Kurki and Tomasz Pietrzykowski (eds) Legal Personhood: Animals, Artificial Intelligence and the Unborn, Springer, E-book, pp. 15–28.

Nash, R. F. (1989). The rights of nature: a history of environmental ethics. Univ of Wisconsin press.

Nash, R. F. (1989). The rights of nature: a history of environmental ethics. Univ of Wisconsin press.

Niezen, R. (2003). The origins of indigenism: Human rights and the politics of identity. Univ of California Press.

O'Donnell, E. (2018). Legal rights for rivers: Competition, collaboration and water governance. Routledge.

O'Donnell, E., Poelina, A., Pelizzon, A., & Clark, C. (2020). Stop Burying the Lede: The Essential Role of Indigenous Law (s) in Creating Rights of Nature. Transnational Environmental Law, 9(3), 403-427.

O'Donnell, E. (2021). Rivers as living beings: rights in law, but no rights to water?. Griffith Law Review, 1-26.

O'Malley, V. (2014). Tūhoe-Crown Settlement-historical background'. Māori Law Review.

Ostrom, E. (1990). Governing the commons: The evolution of institutions for collective action. Cambridge university press.

Patel, G. (2010). Idols in law. Economic and Political Weekly, 47-52.

Rawson, A., & Mansfield, B. (2018). Producing juridical knowledge: "Rights of Nature" or the naturalization of rights?. Environment and Planning E: Nature and Space, 1(1-2), 99-119.

RiverOfLife, M., Poelina, A., Bagnall, D., & Lim, M. (2020). Recognizing the Martuwarra's First Law Right to Life as a Living Ancestral Being. Transnational Environmental Law, 9(3), 541-568.

Robinson, P. J. (1991). Integrity of creation and Christian mission. Missionalia: Southern African Journal of Mission Studies, 19(2), 144-153.

Salmond, A. (2017). Tears of Rangi: Experiments across worlds. Auckland University Press.

Sanders, K. (2018). 'Beyond human ownership'? Property, power and legal personality for nature in Aotearoa New Zealand. Journal of Environmental Law, 30(2), 207-234.

Sands, P. (2016). East West Street. On the Origins of Genocide and Crimes Against Humanity. London: Weidenfeld&Nicolson.
Sanneh, K. (2021). From Guns to Gay Marriage, how did Guns Take over Politics? The New Yorker, May 31 2021 issue.
Serres, M. (1995). The natural contract. University of Michigan Press.
Sharma, N. (2020). Home Rule. Duke University Press.
Simon, F. (2019). La naturaleza como sujeto de derechos en la Constitución ecuatoriana: la construcción de una categoría de interculturalidad (Nature as a Subject of Rights in the Ecuadorian Constitution: The Construction of a Category of Interculturality). La naturaleza como como sujeto de Derechos en el Constitucionalismo Democrático/editores acadé-micos Liliana Estupiñan Achury...[et al.].–Bogotá: Universidad Libre.
Singer, P. (1973). Animal liberation. In Animal Rights (pp. 7-18). Palgrave Macmillan, London.
Skafish, P. (2016a). The Metaphysics of Extra-Moderns: On the Decolonization of Thought—A Conversation with Eduardo Viveiros de Castro. Common Knowledge, 22(3), 393-414.
Skafish, P. (2016b). The Descola variations: The ontological geography of beyond nature and culture. Qui Parle: Critical Humanities and Social Sciences, 25(1-2), 65-93.
Stengers, I. (2010). Cosmopolitics (Vol. 1). Minneapolis: University of Minnesota Press.
Stone, C. (1972). Should trees have standing. Toward Legal Rights for Natural Objects, Souther California Law Review 45, 450-501. .
Stone, C. D. (2010). Should trees have standing?: law, morality, and the environment. Oxford University Press.
Stutzin, G. (1984). Un imperativo ecológico: reconocer los derechos de la naturaleza. Ambiente y Desarrollo, 1(1), 97-114.
Tanas, A., & Gutwirth, S. (2021). Une approche «écologique» des communs dans le droit. Regards sur le patrimoine transpropriatif, les usi civici et la rivière-personne. In Situ. Au regard des sciences sociales.
Tănăsescu, M. (2013). The rights of nature in Ecuador: the making of an idea. International Journal of Environmental Studies, 70(6), 846-861.

Tănăsescu, M. (2014). Rethinking representation: The challenge of non-humans. Australian Journal of Political Science, 49(1), 40-53.

Tănăsescu, M. (2016). Environment, political representation and the challenge of rights: Speaking for Nature. Springer.

Tănăsescu, M. (2020a). Rights of Nature, Legal Personality, and Indigenous Philosophies. Transnational Environmental Law, 9(3), 429-453.

Tănăsescu, M., & Constantinescu, S. (2020b). The human ecology of the Danube Delta: A historical and cartographic perspective. Journal of environmental management, 262, 110324.

Tănăsescu, M. (2022). Ecocene Politics: Mutualism and the Age of Restoration. ...

Tănăsescu, M. (2021) The Rights of Nature as Politics. In Corrigan, D. P., & Oksanen, M. (Eds.), Rights of Nature: a Re-examination, 69-84. London: Routledge.

Tola, M. (2018). Between Pachamama and mother earth: gender, political ontology and the rights of nature in contemporary Bolivia. Feminist review, 118(1), 25-40.

Tzouvala, N. (2020). Capitalism as Civilisation: A History of International Law (Vol. 142). Cambridge University Press.

Van Stekelenburg, J., Roggeband, C., & Klandermans, B. (Eds.). (2013). The future of social movement research: Dynamics, mechanisms, and processes. U of Minnesota Press.

Vasak, K., 1984. 'Pour une troisième generation des droits de l'homme. In Swinarski, C. Ed., Studies and Essays on International Humanitarian Law and Red Cross Principles. International Committee of the Red Cross, Geneva/The Hague: Martinus Nijhoff Publishers.

Stengers, I. (2015). In catastrophic times: Resisting the coming barbarism (p. 156). Open Humanities Press.

Wark, M. (2015). Molecular red: Theory for the Anthropocene. Verso Books.

Waters, C. N., Zalasiewicz, J., Summerhayes, C., Barnosky, A. D., Poirier, C., Gałuszka, A., ... & Wolfe, A. P. (2016). The Anthropocene is functionally and stratigraphically distinct from the Holocene. Science, 351(6269).

Watts, V. (2013). Indigenous place-thought and agency amongst humans and non humans (First Woman and Sky Woman go on a European world tour!). Decolonization: Indigeneity, Education & Society, 2(1).

Zalasiewicz, J., Williams, M., Haywood, A., & Ellis, M. (2011). The Anthropocene: a new epoch of geological time?.

Zalasiewicz, J., Waters, C. N., Williams, M., Barnosky, A. D., Cearreta, A., Crutzen, P., ... & Oreskes, N. (2015). When did the Anthropocene begin? A mid-twentieth century boundary level is stratigraphically optimal. Quaternary International, 383, 196-203.

Social Sciences

kollektiv orangotango+ (ed.)
This Is Not an Atlas
A Global Collection of Counter-Cartographies

2018, 352 p., hardcover, col. ill.
34,99 € (DE), 978-3-8376-4519-4
E-Book: free available, ISBN 978-3-8394-4519-8

Gabriele Dietze, Julia Roth (eds.)
Right-Wing Populism and Gender
European Perspectives and Beyond

April 2020, 286 p., pb., ill.
35,00 € (DE), 978-3-8376-4980-2
E-Book: 34,99 € (DE), ISBN 978-3-8394-4980-6

Mozilla Foundation
Internet Health Report 2019

2019, 118 p., pb., ill.
19,99 € (DE), 978-3-8376-4946-8
E-Book: free available, ISBN 978-3-8394-4946-2

All print, e-book and open access versions of the titles in our list are available in our online shop www.transcript-publishing.com